First World War
and Army of Occupation
War Diary
France, Belgium and Germany

60 DIVISION
Divisional Troops
Royal Army Medical Corps
2/5 London Field Ambulance
1 September 1915 - 28 November 1916

WO95/3029/4

The Naval & Military Press Ltd
www.nmarchive.com
Published in association with The National Archives

Published by

The Naval & Military Press Ltd

Unit 10 Ridgewood Industrial Park,

Uckfield, East Sussex,

TN22 5QE England

Tel: +44 (0) 1825 749494

www.naval-military-press.com

www.nmarchive.com

This diary has been reprinted in facsimile from the original. Any imperfections are inevitably reproduced and the quality may fall short of modern type and cartographic standards.

© **Crown Copyright**
Images reproduced by permission of The National Archives, London, England, 2015.

Contents

Document type	Place/Title	Date From	Date To
Heading	WO95/3029/3		
Heading	60th Division 2-5th London Fld Amb 1915 Sep-1916 Nov		
Heading	War Diary of the 2/5th London Field Ambulance By Major R Corfe Officer Commanding Sept 1st/15 To Sept 30th /15		
War Diary	Hatfield Broad Oak	01/09/1915	30/09/1915
Heading	War Diary of 2/5th Lond Fd Ambulance From Oct 1st/15 Until Oct 31st /15		
War Diary	Hatfield Broad Oak	01/10/1915	29/10/1915
Heading	War Diary of 2/5th London Field Ambulance From Nov 1st/15 To Nov 30th/15		
War Diary	Newport Essex	01/11/1915	30/11/1915
Heading	War Diary of the 2/5th London Field Ambulance From 1st December To 31st December 1915 Volume 12		
War Diary	Newport	01/12/1915	06/12/1915
War Diary	Newport Essex	07/12/1915	31/12/1915
War Diary	Bishops Stortford	16/12/1915	24/12/1915
War Diary	Sutton Veny	01/03/1916	31/03/1916
Miscellaneous	Appendix No.1 Programme of Training		
Miscellaneous	Appendix II Weekly Programme of Training for Week Ending 25.3.16 2/5th London Field Ambulance R.A.M.C.T	21/03/1916	21/03/1916
Miscellaneous	Appendix III Weekly Programme of Training for Week Ending 1.4.16 2/5th London Field Ambulance R.A.M.C. T	25/03/1916	25/03/1916
War Diary	Sutton Veny	01/04/1916	30/04/1916
Miscellaneous	Weekly Programme Of Training For Week Ending 8.4.16 2/5th London Field Ambulance R.A.M.C. T	25/03/1916	25/03/1916
Miscellaneous	Weekly Programme Of Training For Week Ending 15.4.16 2/5th London Field Ambulance R.A.M.C. T	08/04/1916	08/04/1916
Miscellaneous	Weekly Programme Of Training For Week Ending 22.4.16 2/5th London Field Ambulance R.A.M.C. T	15/04/1916	15/04/1916
Miscellaneous	Weekly Programme Of Training For Week Ending 29.4.16 2/5th London Field Ambulance R.A.M.C. T	22/04/1916	22/04/1916
War Diary	Sutton Veny	01/05/1916	31/05/1916
Miscellaneous	Programme of Training for Week Ending 7.5.16 2/5th London Field Ambulance R.A.M.C. T	30/04/1916	30/04/1916
Miscellaneous	Programme of Training For Week Ending 14.5.16 2/5th London Field Ambulance R.A.M.C. T	06/05/1916	06/05/1916
Miscellaneous	Programme of Training for Week Ending 21.5.16 2/5th London Field Ambulance R.A.M.C. T	13/05/1916	13/05/1916
Miscellaneous	2/5th London Field Ambulance Programme Of Training For Week-Ending 28-5-16	20/05/1916	20/05/1916
Miscellaneous	60th Divisional Exercise-26th May 1916	26/05/1916	26/05/1916
Heading	60th Div 2/5th London Field Ambulance June 1916		
War Diary	Sutton Veny	01/06/1916	04/06/1916
War Diary	Wilts	05/06/1916	09/06/1916
War Diary	Sutton Veny	10/06/1916	15/06/1916
War Diary	Sutton Veny, Wilts	16/06/1916	23/06/1916

War Diary	Le Havre	24/06/1916	25/06/1916
War Diary	Hericourt	26/06/1916	27/06/1916
War Diary	Penin	28/06/1916	30/06/1916
Miscellaneous	Programme of Training for Week Ending 4.6.15 2/5th London Field Ambulance R.A.M.C. T.	27/05/1916	27/05/1916
Miscellaneous	Programme of Training for Week Ending 11.6.15 2/5th London Field Ambulance R.A.M.C. T.	02/06/1916	02/06/1916
Miscellaneous	Programme of Training for Week Ending 17.6.15 2/5th London Field Ambulance R.A.M.C. T.	10/06/1916	10/06/1916
Miscellaneous	Programme of Training for Week Ending		
Heading	War Diary of 2/5th London Field Ambulance From July 1st 1916 To July 31st 1916 Vol II		
War Diary	Penin	01/07/1916	01/07/1916
War Diary	Tinquette	02/07/1916	12/07/1916
War Diary	Haute-Avesnes	13/07/1916	31/07/1916
Heading	War Diary of 2/5th London Field Ambulance From August 1st 1916 To August 31st 1916 Vol 3		
War Diary	Haute-Avesnes	03/08/1916	31/08/1916
Heading	60th Div War Diary of 2/5th London Field Ambulance From September 1st 1916 To September 30th 1916 Vol 4		
War Diary	Haute-Avesnes	03/09/1916	29/09/1916
Heading	60th Div 2/5 London Field Ambulance Oct 1916		
Heading	War Diary of 2/5th London Field Ambulance From October 1st 1916 To October 31st 1916 Vol 5		
War Diary	Haute-Avesnes	01/10/1916	23/10/1916
War Diary	Penin	24/10/1916	25/10/1916
War Diary	Moncheaux	26/10/1916	27/10/1916
War Diary	Remaisnil	28/10/1916	28/10/1916
War Diary	Le Meillard	29/10/1916	31/10/1916
Heading	War Diary 2/5th London Field Ambulance October 1st-October 31st 1916		
Operation(al) Order(s)	180th Infantry Brigade Order No.18	23/10/1916	23/10/1916
Miscellaneous	March Table		
Miscellaneous	O.C. 2/5th Field London Field Ambulance	25/10/1916	25/10/1916
Operation(al) Order(s)	180th Infantry Brigade Order No.19	27/10/1916	27/10/1916
Miscellaneous	March Table		
Operation(al) Order(s)	180th Infantry Brigade Order No.20	28/10/1916	28/10/1916
Miscellaneous	March Table		
Operation(al) Order(s)	R.A.M.C. Operation Order No.3	20/10/1916	20/10/1916
Operation(al) Order(s)	60th Division R.A.M.C. Operation Order No.4	22/10/1916	22/10/1916
Miscellaneous	Relief Table Of Field Ambulances Of 60th (London) Division		
Miscellaneous	Table "D"		
Heading	War Diary of 2/5th London Field Ambulance R.A.M.C. T From November 1st 1916 To November 30th 1916		
War Diary	Le Meillard	01/11/1916	02/11/1916
War Diary	Bussus-Bussuel	03/11/1916	20/11/1916
War Diary	Marseilles	21/11/1916	22/11/1916
War Diary	Marseilles (Musso)	22/11/1916	28/11/1916
War Diary	H.M.T Ivernia At Sea	28/11/1916	28/11/1916
Miscellaneous	180th Infantry Brigade March Table	18/11/1916	18/11/1916

WO 95/3029/3

60TH DIVISION

2-5TH LONDON FLD AMB

~~JUN~~ ~~OV 1915~~

1915 SEP — 1916 NOV

Confidential

War Diary
of the 2/5th Lond. Field Ambulance
by Major R. Cope
Officer Commanding

Sept 1st/15 to Sept 30th/15.

Army Form C. 2118.

WAR DIARY
or
INTELLIGENCE SUMMARY.

2/5" Mounted Field Ambulance
#180" Infantry Bde.
60-Lord New Zealand

(Erase heading not required.)

Instructions regarding War Diaries and Intelligence Summaries are contained in F.S. Regs., Part II. and the Staff Manual respectively. Title pages will be prepared in manuscript.

Hour, Date, Place	Summary of Events and Information	Remarks and references to Appendices
Hatfield Broad Oak		
Sept 1st 1915. 6 p.m.	L/C Lambert has been detailed (with 2 w men) to attend a course of instruction in Transport Duties. They were despatched yesterday to Saffron Walden for this purpose & attached temporarily to the "1/1st" 2/4" Field Ambulance. —	A.C.
Sept 3rd	Two horses of this unit are in isolation, suspected of mange. Weather has been very cold recently. —	A.C.
Sept 5th	Sanitation of the Camps is good & kept well in control. The general health of the camps remains good, though there are still a number of cases of scabies constantly recurring. I have not yet been able to get the Huearts desinfector repaired. —	A.C.

(73969) W4141—463. 400,000. 9/14. H.&J.Ltd. Forms/C. 2118/10.

WAR DIARY

Army Form C. 2118.

INTELLIGENCE SUMMARY

(Erase heading not required.)

2/1st London Field Ambulance —
1st S.D. Bde. 60th Lond. Div.

Instructions regarding War Diaries and Intelligence Summaries are contained in F.S. Regs., Part II. and the Staff Manual respectively. Title pages will be prepared in manuscript.

Hour, Date, Place	Summary of Events and Information	Remarks and references to Appendices
Hospital Broad Oak —		
6 p.m. Sept 7th 1915.	Lt Lambert & the 2 men who have been attending a course of instruction at Saffron Walden returned to-day. The Horsfall Destructor is working very well, but is rapidly wearing out; the interior brickwork has become loose & fallen away, several internal metal parts have become fused & melted, also a large crack has occurred in the external metal framework of the furnace — the Destructor has been in use not much longer than six or seven weeks.	A.C.
Sept 9th.	A great deal of firing (probably by anti-aircraft guns) was heard last night, about midnight.	R.C.
Sept 10th.	Major Macaulay is confined to bed with arthritis? of the left knee —
I have been ordered by the A.D.M.S. to issue a great deal of Medical & Surgical equipment to other units of the Division.	R.C.

Army Form C. 2118.

WAR DIARY
INTELLIGENCE SUMMARY
(Erase heading not required.)

2/5th Lond. Field Ambulance
180th Inf. Bde. = 60th Lond. Divn.

Instructions regarding War Diaries and Intelligence Summaries are contained in F.S. Regs., Part II. and the Staff Manual respectively. Title pages will be prepared in manuscript.

Hour, Date, Place	Summary of Events and Information	Remarks and references to Appendices
Ht Field Broad Oak		
6 p.m. Sept 11th, 1915.	I, in common with other units of this Brigade, have been ordered to column all ex-Home tents with distemper.	R.C.
Sept 13th	R.A.M.C. men for water duties are now being sent from this unit to replace men who left the Battalions of this Brigade on separation of the Home-service men.	R.C.
Sept 14th	The issues of Medl. & Surg. equipment which I have been ordered to make are almost completed, & I have little more than the equipment of one Section remaining. The equipment is very old, in bad condition, & has J.P. defects. This is as it was received by me.	R.C.
Sept 15th	Although not recovered, Major Macaulay is again on duty. Field training is now carried out twice a week in conjunction with the Regimental Medl. Stabls turned of one or more of the Battalions of this Brigade. To-day we were visited in the field by the A.D.M.S.	R.C.

WAR DIARY
or
INTELLIGENCE SUMMARY.
(Erase heading not required.)

Army Form C. 2118.

2/1st London Field Ambulance
180th Infantry Bde. 60th (London) Divn.

Hour, Date, Place	Summary of Events and Information	Remarks and references to Appendices
Hatfield Broad Oak 6 pm. Sept 17th 1916.	A considerable number of cases have recently been examined & classified by the Standing Medical Board, the men coming from units of this Brigade	R.C.
Sept 18th	Capt. Naylor sustained a ? of his wrist, & ? of a severe accident last night, when returning from Bishops Stortford. The seat of a waggon the in which he was riding became loose & fell over the side, Capt. Naylor fell with it & fractured the base of his skull. He was taken at once to the Civilian Hospital at Bishops Stortford – He is doing as well as can be expected — R.C.
Sept 21st & 22nd —	A regimental Court of Enquiry was held on the accident to Capt. Naylor — (nobody to blame)	R.C.
Sept 22nd	The unit was inspected this afternoon in camp by the D.D.M.S. 3rd Army. Every thorough inspection.	R.C.

WAR DIARY
INTELLIGENCE SUMMARY
(Erase heading not required.)

Army Form C. 2118.

2/5th London Field Ambulance
180th Inf. Bde., 1st Bde. —
60th London Divn.

Instructions regarding War Diaries and Intelligence Summaries are contained in F.S. Regs., Part II. and the Staff Manual respectively. Title pages will be prepared in manuscript.

Hour, Date, Place	Summary of Events and Information	Remarks and references to Appendices
Magpie Broad Estb.		
6 p.m. Sept 26th 1915.	Night exercises in the trenches (dug by Battalions of this Brigade) were carried out last night [?].	R.C.
Sept 27th	Orderly room work (returns, accounts, indents, general queries & correspondence) seems to increase more & more, & takes much of my attention away from the training of the unit, especially as I am now without an Aux. Sermanser — Most returns seem to be required by the Officer Commanding, the Brigade as well as by the A.D.M.S. —	R.C.
Sept 28th — Sept 30th —	Inspection of transport by O.C. A.S.C. 60th Lond. Divn. — Anti-typhoid inoculation of recent recruits now completed. There is never any difficulty in this unit in inducing the men to consent to this procedure —	R.C. R.C.

Confidential.

War Diary

2/5th (?) Field Ambulance

from Oct 1st 6/15 — until Oct 31st/15

ACR? Major
C 2/5 2d Wes Amb

Army Form C. 2118.

WAR DIARY
INTELLIGENCE SUMMARY.

(Erase heading not required.)

2/5: London Field Ambulance.
180: Inf. Bde.
6a = toward, Div =

Instructions regarding War Diaries and Intelligence Summaries are contained in F.S. Regs., Part II. and the Staff Manual respectively. Title pages will be prepared in manuscript.

Hour, Date, Place	Summary of Events and Information	Remarks and references to Appendices
Hd Qrs field Broad Oak 6 p.m. Oct. 1st 1915.	This unit took part in a Divisional exercise by the 180" x 181" Brigades against a skeleton enemy. Position of enemy was at Easton Lodge – Roke – Mount Pleasant. Station was formed by this unit at Canfield Hall, S.W. of Takely. Lower buildings being utilised for the purpose. R.C. The Church Strangletow is at S. End in working order, &	R.C.
Oct 2nd	The horse boys recently received on charge were disinfected to-day. The weather has been very cold recently.	R.C.
Oct 4th	Received orders to-day for a Divisional exercise commencing to-morrow & extending over four days. Have been made preparations to-day.	R.C.
Oct 5th – 8th	Divisional exercise:– 5th: This unit proceeded by route march to Hare St. with	

WAR DIARY

INTELLIGENCE SUMMARY

Army Form C. 2118.

2/5" London Fd. Amb.
180" Inf. Bde.
60" London Div.

(Erase heading not required.)

Instructions regarding War Diaries and Intelligence Summaries are contained in F.S. Regs., Part II. and the Staff Manual respectively. Title pages will be prepared in manuscript.

Hour, Date, Place	Summary of Events and Information	Remarks and references to Appendices
Hatfield Bd. Oak Oct. 9th 6 p.m.	The 180th Bde. & Bivouacked in Langley Park for the night.	
6th	The Bde. advanced to White Notley & occupied the trenches from Hazebrook Green to Longer Hall for the night. This unit went into Bivouacs at White Notley.	
7th	The enemy having been strongly reinforced, the Bde. retired to Hoo 8th, & resistance ceased. Some units were billeted in Little Baddow, this unit again went into bivouacs at Langley Park.	
8th	The Bde. returned to Camp at Hatfield Broad Oak. Weather has been very good during the exercise.	
Oct 9th	There are now 36 cases of scabies in hospital. They have accumulated owing to the difficulty & delay in obtaining Balsam of Peru & Sulphur ointment. This disease seemed to start in the 2/17 Bn. & 2/18 Bns.; It has spread to the 2/15	

WAR DIARY
INTELLIGENCE SUMMARY

Army Form C. 2118.

7/5 Lond. Fd Amb—
180 Inf. Bde.
60 Lond. Divt

Hour, Date, Place	Summary of Events and Information	Remarks and references to Appendices
Hospital B.E. Ook 6/7 mo		
Oct 11/17	O.T. has now opened to the 7/197. There seem to be clear evidence of severe billious in existence of this disease accompanying every move on Divisional exer- cise involving an extreme wide weather of Blacked R.E.	
Oct 12/17	Frequent medical boards deemed on good deal of time from the 3 Medical Officers of this unit. Officers of this unit took part in a Divisional Staff ride in neighbourhood of Farnham, Maunders etc., in prepar- ation for a Divisional exercise with troops in the same area to taken place on Oct 14th. Another Medical Board to day.	R.E. R.E.
Oct 13	Aircraft heard & seen over this camp about 9.0 p.m. 2 Zeppelins. Both at considerable height & distance.	R.E.

WAR DIARY
INTELLIGENCE SUMMARY

Army Form C. 2118.

Instructions regarding War Diaries and Intelligence Summaries are contained in F.S. Regs., Part II and the Staff Manual respectively. Title pages will be prepared in manuscript.

(Erase heading not required.)

2/5th Lonl. Fd. Amb.
180th Inf. Bde.
60th Lond. Divn

Hour, Date, Place	Summary of Events and Information	Remarks and references to Appendices
Heyfield Bard Camp 6 p.m. Oct 14th – 15th	This wasn't took part in a Divisional exercise, being attacked by the 180th Bde. The enemy was retiring on line of Heydes abv. the river Ath. this Divin held offensive trenches on a line from the Ford south of Furness Pellamin & Citygate, & the 180th Bde. were to attack the enemy trenches opposite the northern bank of their line after 2 hours bombardment by our Artillery. A special exercise was that this Field Amb. in that 10% of the troops were detailed & ordered to fall out as casualties, these were (211.) were brought in by the Bearer Divn. to a main dressing station at Shamshead (clear well kept) from buildings having been prepared carefully by the Sanity Divn., were handed over to Tent section, given treatment & detained for the night – Seriously ill cases again attended to their own officers (colors. Cosens & Capt.) R.C. given then the next morning (15 Oct), & they were then sent back to camp and in their own ??? very well executed throughout	

WAR DIARY
INTELLIGENCE SUMMARY

Army Form C. 2118.

2/5 London Fd Ambulance
180th Inf Bde
60th L. Div

Hour, Date, Place	Summary of Events and Information	Remarks and references to Appendices
Hatfield Rd Sch 6 pm Oct 18th	Scabies cases still continue to be admitted to Hospital. The Hospital Blankets have all been disinfected & we are now disinfecting all Blankets of this unit - not more than 25 can be done at one time in the Thresh disinfector. Report rec'd. ℔ R.D.M.S. re occurrence of scabies in the Bde AC.	R.C. R.C.
Oct 19th – 22nd	This unit took part in a Divisional exercise extending over 4 days:— 1st day. – Advanced with 180th Inf Bde. To assistance of the 107th Provisional Bde. against an enemy who had landed at "The Naze" + were advancing in a south-westerly direction. took up close billets for the night at Honor St. + the Walthams; this unit being established at Langley's Park. 2nd day. Advanced towards White Notley, But on the route news was received that the enemy had been reinforced + had landed outside the 107th Provis. Bde., this Bde. was ordered to divert its route to the south & occupy trenches from	Ref. 1/2 π O.S. No 30.

WAR DIARY
INTELLIGENCE SUMMARY

Army Form C. 2118.

1/5 London Field Amb.
180 Infy. Bde.
60 Lond. Divn.

Hour, Date, Place	Summary of Events and Information	Remarks and references to Appendices
	Then Rt. in Ravenhall to the G.E.R. line north of the C. in Chipping Hill – A main dressing station was selected at Jenkins Place, during Collecting Stations at Fulbro St., during station for the 6th Fd. Amb. was also at Jenkins Place, that for the 4th Fd. Amb. at Bryers Farm. The Bearer Divn. was sent forward. The 3rd Amb. Bivouacked at Jenkins Place. — 3rd day. The Division advanced, acting as rear guard covering the retirement of an army. This unit retired in advance of the 180th Bde. Keeping in touch at about 1/2 to 1 mile distant. The 4th Amb. again went into the close billets at Langley Park. Operations ceased. 4th day. Troops returned to camp at Hatfield Broad Oak. There are still a large no. of men who fell out from sore feet on the line of march. but a considerable improvement is noted, especially when the Fd. Amb. Lambs. wagons are in front of the troops instead of behind them. R.E.	During this research D. Hill - A main received, the great recovery In Field Kitchens for a Field Ambulance has very clearly shewn, not only for men of the unit, but for Fds. Amb. thought to, a footrest up on the line of march. R.E.

Army Form C. 2118.

WAR DIARY
or
INTELLIGENCE SUMMARY.
(Erase heading not required.)

Instructions regarding War Diaries and Intelligence Summaries are contained in F.S. Regs., Part II. and the Staff Manual respectively. Title pages will be prepared in manuscript.

Hour, Date, Place	Summary of Events and Information	Remarks and references to Appendices
Hatfield Broad Oak		
6 p.m. Oct 22nd/15.	Medical Board ("standing") held on Capn J. Groves -	RC
" 23rd "	Packing up. definite orders having been received that the Bde. move by road to Saffron Walden on Oct 26th/15.	RC
" 24th "	6 G.S. wagons sent by A.S.C. to assist in moving equipment.	RC
" 25th "	Moved at 8 a.m. Convoy near front, (1 N.C.O. 10 men) arrived at Newport at 11.30 a.m. from Newport, 3 miles from Saffron Walden has been allotted to this unit as its billeting area -	RC
" 27th "	The unit has settled down, normal course of Training has been resumed. The Bdr. by arrangement of A.D.M.S., left all blankets at Hatfield Bde Gate for disinfection & cleaning. Being issued with new blankets at Saffron Walden - this with a view to checking scabies -	RC
" 29th "	Conference of Officers at Bishop's Stortford on recent Divisional exercise. Making of medical Officers generals at A.D.M.S. Office for same purpose -	RC

Confidential

War Diary
of
2/5th London Field Ambulance

From Nov- 1st/15 to Nov- 30th/15

for Major R. Cox Ra.
OC 2/5 L.F. Amb.

WAR DIARY
INTELLIGENCE SUMMARY.
(Erase heading not required.)

Army Form C. 2118.

2/5 Bn. 1st Lt Amb[ulance]
60th London Div[ision]

Hour, Date, Place	Summary of Events and Information	Remarks and references to Appendices
Newport Essex		
6 p.m. Nov 1st 1915.	My Quartermaster, Captn. Naylor, is still absent on sick leave, & I have to take on his duties as far as possible. In addition I find the Orderly Room work occupies on an average at least 4 hours of my time daily. The two Medical Officers under my command are employed one in charge of the Hospital & one to work with the men (for training).	R.C.
Nov 2nd 3 1/2	Summoned to Bishops Stortford to meet ADMS. The Officer to discuss how reinforcements to Bn. of 12 men there should be dealt with. Went on to Hatfield Broad Oak to inspect new party Sgt Kerr under Sergt Gillard & picked up stores &c for us at Sawbridgeworth & Takeley, returning	R.C.
"" "" 12""		
Nov 4th	This much Battn. Took part in a Divisional exercise, accompanying the 180th Bde. in an advance on Stansted (n Bower Rd on Bde.) acting as Forms/C. 2118/10.] a strong advanced guard of the Bde.	R.C.

WAR DIARY

INTELLIGENCE SUMMARY

2/5th Lond. Fd. Amb.
60th Lond. Divn.

Army Form C. 2118.

(Erase heading not required.)

Hour, Date, Place	Summary of Events and Information	Remarks and references to Appendices
Watford. 6 p.m. Nov 6th/15.	Orderly Room work still very excessive, many returns have to be sent in to the Bde. as well as to the A.D.M.S. — A.B. 480 — has been wrongly made out & has to be re-written, the "forage & animal a/c" & the "sack a/c" has also given considerable worry & anxiety. —	R.C.
Nov 8th	Medical Board at "The Crown Hotel" —	R.C.
Nov 10th	Inspection by L.O.C. 60th Lond. Divn. who devoted his attention chiefly to the messing Billets & cook-house — Medical Board in Bishops Stafford (Pte. Botham J.) Night operations carried out by the unit.	R.C.
Nov: 12th	The unit has not yet been able to secure latrines & ablution benches, which are urgently required for the troops. Hospital, Transport section & all other personnel used by the unit — Concerts are being held "weekly" in the Village Hall, which the men are allowed to use as a recreation room —	R.C. V.C.

WAR DIARY

INTELLIGENCE SUMMARY

2/5- Lond. Field Amb.
60- Lond. Div.

Army Form C. 2118.

Instructions regarding War Diaries and Intelligence Summaries are contained in F.S. Regs., Part II. and the Staff Manual respectively. Title pages will be prepared in manuscript.

(Erase heading not required.)

Hour, Date, Place	Summary of Events and Information	Remarks and references to Appendices
Newport Essex.		
6 p.m. Nov. 13th	Many of the Horses left behind at HATFIELD BROAD OAK have now been returned, camp equipment & O.O. CHELMSFORD other equipment brought back here. Six of the men (of the rear party) have returned here, leaving S/Serg. BILLARD & 4 men still at HATFIELD 13th OAK.	R.C.
Nov. 14th	A List of N.C.O.s & men for promotion has been approved by the A.D.M.S., we were being deficient in establishment of Sergeants.	R.C.
Nov. 15th	Med. Board in large number of men of the 2/17th Battn. Lond. Reg.	R.C.
Nov. 16th	Heavy fall of snow last night.	R.C.
Nov. 17th	Snow travelled interferes with the training programme. Consolation night march carried out under N.C.O.s tonight.	R.C.
Nov. 18th	Capt. MAYCOR has today returned to duty, after his accident.	R.C.
Nov. 19th	Inspection by the A.D.M.S. of the whole 3rd Ambulance this morning, the men being subsequently addressed by him. (Goodwood have 9 skulls first 9 weeks ago)	R.C.

WAR DIARY
INTELLIGENCE SUMMARY

Army Form C. 2118.

75th Lond. Fd Amb"
60" Lond Div"

(Erase heading not required.)

Instructions regarding War Diaries and Intelligence Summaries are contained in F. S. Regs., Part II. and the Staff Manual respectively. Title pages will be prepared in manuscript.

Hour, Date, Place	Summary of Events and Information	Remarks and references to Appendices
NEWPORT ESSEX.		
6 p.m. Nov 19th (continued)	Med: Board this afternoon on Major FRANKLIN, 2/20th Bde" & a man from Bde.	
Nov 20th	Stores Coy behind at BRAINTREE were to a great extent cleared yesterday, 160 Blankets were sent to D.D. COLCHESTER & be cleaned, a considerable amount of equipment was transferred to the 76th Fd Amb" (stationed at BRAINTREE) by order of A.D.M.S – a considerable amount was brought back here by regimental transport – The 75th Blankets Coy at HATFIELD 13° OAK have now been sent to D.A.D.O.S. (to be cleaned), the remainder of the Coys equipment has been sent to D.O.O. CHELMSFORD, all remaining Stores being left there – S'Sergt & remaining 4 men of the rear party have to-day reported here –	R.C. R.C. R.C.
Nov 21st	There is still snow on high lying ground, & the weather remains cold –	R.C.

Army Form C. 2118.

WAR DIARY
~~INTELLIGENCE SUMMARY~~

2/5th Lond, Fd Amb[?]
60th Lond, Div[?]

(Erase heading not required.)

Instructions regarding War Diaries and Intelligence Summaries are contained in F.S. Regs., Part II and the Staff Manual respectively. Title pages will be prepared in manuscript.

Hour, Date, Place	Summary of Events and Information	Remarks and references to Appendices
NEWPORT.		
6 p.m. Nov. 22nd 1915.	Cases of scabies still occur in the 180th Inf. Bde. & are admitted to the Reception Hospital of this unit. Med. Board this afternoon — 7/20.	R.C.
Nov. 23rd	The remainder of the Stores of Braintree have been brought back here by regimental transport to-day. Med. Board this afternoon — 3/19.	R.C.
Nov. 24th	Weather still keeps very cold. 27 Ground sheets are reported missing.	R.C.
Nov. 25th	Orders have been issued that the Transport Section of Field Ambulances are to be transferred to the A.S.C. Med. Board this afternoon — 3/17.	R.C.
Nov. 26th	Training carried on as usual in accordance with weekly programme, though owing to pressure of Orderly Room work, & to the vacancy of Hospital duty, only one Officer frequently is available to go out with the men.	R.C.

WAR DIARY
INTELLIGENCE SUMMARY

Army Form C. 2118.

2/5- Lond, Fld Ambulance
60- London Div—

Hour, Date, Place	Summary of Events and Information	Remarks and references to Appendices
NEWPORT.		
6p.m. Nov 27th Nov 28th	Weather still very cold. 12 degrees of frost last night— Church Parade at NEWPORT Church as usual. The men are now having 4 days leave, 10% at a time in accordance with permission given (orders A5)	RC. RC.
Nov. 29th	Men of Brigade examined by the Inspecting Dental Officer at the Hospital (by appointments) .—	RC.
Nov. 30th	Weather a little warmer— Med. Board this afternoon—	RC.

ACox Major
O/C 2/5- Lond. Fld Amb.

C O N F I D E N T I A L.

WAR DIARY of the

2/5th LONDON FIELD AMBULANCE.

From 1st DECEMBER to 31st DECEMBER 1915.

VOLUME 12.

Army Form C. 2118.

WAR DIARY
or
INTELLIGENCE SUMMARY
(Erase heading not required.)

2/5 London Field Ambulance
60th (London) Division

Instructions regarding War Diaries and Intelligence Summaries are contained in F. S. Regs., Part II. and the Staff Manual respectively. Title pages will be prepared in manuscript.

Hour, Date, Place	Summary of Events and Information	Remarks and references to Appendices
NEWPORT		
6 p.m. Dec. 1st/15.	Rain – Night exercises carried out –	R.C.
" 2nd "	The cottage hitherto occupied as a scabies hospital has been found to be too small & another house has to-day been taken for the purpose –	R.C.
" 3rd "	More rain – Medical Board this afternoon – Consent for move to single.	R.C.
" 4th "	Heavy downpour of rain all day – Special entraining & detraining exercise (repeated after dark) at Saltram Walden chiefly for horses & wagons, arranged for this unit by the Brigade, under supervision of Capt. SAUNDERS, 2/5 Bn RA –	R.C.
" 5th "	Church parade as usual –	R.C.
" 6th "	More rain –	R.C.

Army Form C. 2118.

WAR DIARY
INTELLIGENCE SUMMARY.
(Erase heading not required.)

3/5th London Field Ambulance
60th (London) Division

Instructions regarding War Diaries and Intelligence Summaries are contained in F.S. Regs., Part II. and the Staff Manual respectively. Title pages will be prepared in manuscript.

Hour, Date, Place	Summary of Events and Information	Remarks and references to Appendices
NEWPORT ESSEX		
6 p.m. Dec 7th 1915.	Training carried on as usual, though the Country around is flooded & very muddy — Medical Board this afternoon —	R.C.
Dec 8th	Two Mark A.S.S. wagons issued to the Unit in place of unserviceable civilian wagons — Night Rt exercises carried out —	R.C.
Dec 9th	Inspection of Unit by A.D.M.S. Medical Board this afternoon —	R.C.
Dec 10th	One Sergeant, 2 rank & File have been sent to Mrs t. Bart's Hospital at Denmark Hill for 3 weeks training in the wards —	R.C.
Dec 11th	Inspecting Dental Officer attended to examine men of this Brigade —	R.C.
Dec 12th	Church Parade —	R.C.

Army Form C. 2118.

WAR DIARY
INTELLIGENCE SUMMARY.
2/5" London Field Ambulance
60" (2nd London) Div"
(Erase heading not required.)

Instructions regarding War Diaries and Intelligence Summaries are contained in F.S. Regs., Part II. and the Staff Manual respectively. Title pages will be prepared in manuscript.

Hour, Date, Place	Summary of Events and Information	Remarks and references to Appendices
NEWPORT ESSEX.		
4 p.m. Dec 13"	Medical Board this afternoon —	R.C.
Dec 14"	Very cold during the last few days. Regimental Board on "old clothing"	R.C.
Dec 15"	D.A.D.O.S. visited unit to inspect "old clothing" & interview able bearer —	R.C.
Dec 16"	Night exercises held. Aim — to turn given in places of fire. air drawing	R.C. R.C.
Dec 17"	"Board" (regimental) held to examine equipment in possession & compare with kit held in charge — Mr Martin Harvey & a party gave an evening entertainment to the men —	R.C. R.C.
Dec 18"	Cases of scabies still frequently occur in the 180" L.F. Reg.	R.C.
Dec 19"	Church Parade —	R.C.

WAR DIARY
INTELLIGENCE SUMMARY
(Erase heading not required.)

Army Form C. 2118.

2/5th London Field Ambulance
60th (London) Division.

Hour, Date, Place	Summary of Events and Information	Remarks and references to Appendices
NEWPORT – ESSEX.		
Dec 24th/15. 6 p.m.	Med: exam:s of all Personnel continued to-day. – Personnel of Transport Section with the exception of S/S Lindsell & Corpl. were today transferred to the Army Service Corps, in accordance with orders received. Another case (no such case?) received this morning (Baseoff A.D.M.S.)	R.C.
Dec 25th (Xmas Day)	A gracious Xmas message from His Majesty the KING was received through the Bde. & read out on Parade. Church Parade. – Xmas dinner in Village Hall (Officers & men all dined together.)	R.C.
Dec 26th	Chapel Parade. –	
Dec 27th	Holiday by permission of G.O.C. – Football match (Barnes v. Frankfurt) in morning – Entertainment in Village Hall in evening. –	R.C.

WAR DIARY
INTELLIGENCE SUMMARY
(Erase heading not required.)

Army Form C. 2118.

1/3rd London Field Ambulance
60th (2nd) Division

Hour, Date, Place	Summary of Events and Information	Remarks and references to Appendices
NEWPORT ESSEX. 6/1 — Dec 20th 1915	Route march. Foot, Boot & Kit inspection in afternoon.	R.C.
" 21st	Field training. Two more G.S. wagons, marquee &c, received.	R.C.
" 22nd	Inspection this morning with other units of the 180th Bde, 179th Bde by the newly appointed G.O.C. Div., Maj. Gen. BULFIN. L.A.D.M.S. & Brigadier General on SAFFRON WALDEN Common.	R.C.
" 23rd	My orders received by wire (through Bates) for immediate medical exam" of Officers & men, to test & report on fitness to serve abroad (numbers 87 to be wired Asst. to Secretary, Con.D. Jones, 3rd Army, & Divt. Examin" begun this evening; & wires despatched to asked for exam" of 87 & report on men being detached (on various courses)	R.C.

Army Form C. 2118.

2/5th Lond: Field Ambulance
60th (2nd Lond) Division

WAR DIARY
INTELLIGENCE SUMMARY.
(Erase heading not required.)

Instructions regarding War Diaries and Intelligence Summaries are contained in F.S. Regs., Part II. and the Staff Manual respectively. Title pages will be prepared in manuscript.

Hour, Date, Place	Summary of Events and Information	Remarks and references to Appendices
NEWPORT ESSEX		
Dec 28th 6 p.m.	Route march - 14 miles - no men fell out.	R.C.
Dec 29th	Night exercises.	R.C.
Dec 30th	Field training - Hospital visited & inspected by the A.D.M.S.	R.C.
Dec 31st	Board of inquiry on equipment's missing - Medical Board - 1 Sergt & 1 man reported back from convalescent Ho at Lords Gen'l Hosp'l.	R.C.

RC Lee
Major 2nd Lond F. Ambulance
O/c 2/5th Lond: F. Ambulance

WAR DIARY
or
INTELLIGENCE SUMMARY.
(Erase heading not required.)

Army Form C. 2118.

Instructions regarding War Diaries and Intelligence Summaries are contained in F.S. Regs., Part II. and the Staff Manual respectively. Title pages will be prepared in manuscript.

Hour, Date, Place	Summary of Events and Information	Remarks and references to Appendices

Army Form C. 2118.

WAR DIARY
or
INTELLIGENCE SUMMARY.
(Erase heading not required.)

Instructions regarding War Diaries and Intelligence Summaries are contained in F.S. Regs., Part II. and the Staff Manual respectively. Title pages will be prepared in manuscript.

2/5TH LONDON FIELD AMBULANCE

Hour, Date, Place	Summary of Events and Information	Remarks and references to Appendices
Sutton Veney		
March 1 1916 6pm	Programme of Training as appended by A.D.M.S.	Appendix I W/m
March 2 6pm	Outdoor Training greatly hampered by bad weather — some having to be carried out in the huts	W/m
March 3 8pm	Programme of Training as appended by A.D.M.S.	Appendix I W/m
March 4 8pm	do	do W/m
	Precautions against fire arrived and improved	W/m
March 5 6pm	Church Parade to Sutton Veney Church	W/m
March 6 6pm	A heavy fall of snow during the night has necessitated training taking place in the Huts	W/m
March 7 6pm	Still snowing — Training in Huts	
8pm	An experimental trial of extinguishing all lights took place between 7 and 7.20 and as regards this hut was completely successful	W/m

Army Form C. 2118.

WAR DIARY
or
~~INTELLIGENCE SUMMARY~~

(Erase heading not required.)

Hour, Date, Place	Summary of Events and Information	Remarks and references to Appendices
Sutton Veny March 7 1916 cont^d	Capt C. Burrows having been transferred to this unit from the 2/1st Battⁿ L.R. is taken on the strength as from Feb 28 1916 and is posted to "C" Section	W/W
March 8 6 p.m.	Training Programme as appended by A.D.M.S.	appendix I W/W
	Special order issued as to Smoking on the march.	W/W
	Lieut F.C. Morris R.A.M.C. reported for duty	
March 9 6 p.m.	Weather improved – Route march (Company?) Capt R.E. Stoke-Brockman having reported for duty is taken on the strength of this unit as from March 7 1916	
	Capt C. Burrows granted extension of sick leave until march 13 1916	W/W
March 10 6 p.m.	Training according to Programme appended by A.D.M.S	appendix I

(73989) W4141—463. 400,000. 9/14. H.&J.Ltd. Forms/C. 2118/10.

WAR DIARY or INTELLIGENCE SUMMARY

Army Form C. 2118.

(Erase heading not required.)

Hour, Date, Place		Summary of Events and Information	Remarks and references to Appendices
Sutton Veny March 11 1916	6 p.m.	Special training programme of A.D.M.S. In accordance with Divisional Letter A/226/3 of 8th March 1916 Special Precautions against Fire again issued in Regimental Orders	Appendix I
March 12	6 p.m. 8 p.m.	Sutton Veny Church for service. Lieut C.R. Horrod R.A.M.C. having returned for duty is taken on the strength of this unit	13/3/16
March 13	8 p.m.	Route march and training according to weekly programme drawn up & submitted to A.D.M.S.	Appendix II 13/3/16
		do	13/3/16
March 14	6 p.m.	Lecture on Anti-Gas helmets by Capt. Athcar attended by 3 officers and 4 N.C.O.	13/3/16

Army Form C. 2118.

WAR DIARY
or
INTELLIGENCE SUMMARY.
(Erase heading not required.)

Instructions regarding War Diaries and Intelligence Summaries are contained in F.S. Regs., Part II. and the Staff Manual respectively. Title pages will be prepared in manuscript.

Hour, Date, Place	Summary of Events and Information	Remarks and references to Appendices
Sutton Veney		
March 15 1916 6pm	Training in accordance with weekly Programme Lecture on Antigas matters by Capt. Cathcart attended by remaining foe Officers	appendix II W/W
March 16 6pm	Route March (Longleat Park) - Other training in accordance with weekly Programme	appendix II
9pm	The following postings take effect from today A Section - Capt C Burrows B Section Lieut R C Horsman C Section Capt R E. Drake-Brockman Lieut F C Warren Lieut R C Horsman has been ordered to report to British East Africa Barrack Stores in all the huts checked	W/W

WAR DIARY or INTELLIGENCE SUMMARY

Army Form C. 2118.

(Erase heading not required.)

Instructions regarding War Diaries and Intelligence Summaries are contained in F.S. Regs., Part II. and the Staff Manual respectively. Title pages will be prepared in manuscript.

25TH LONDON FIELD AMBULANCE

Hour, Date, Place	Summary of Events and Information	Remarks and references to Appendices
Sutton Veny		
March 17 1916 6pm	Training in accordance with weekly programme. All Chimneys swept.	Appendix II W/m
March 18 6pm	Training in accordance with weekly programme	W/m
March 19 6pm	Service in Sutton Veny Church	W/m
March 20 6pm	Training in accordance with weekly programme	W/m appendix II
March 21 6pm	do do	W/m do
March 22 6pm	do do	W/m do
March 23 6pm	do do	W/m do
	Capt. ?O?. Stedman detailed with 1 NCO and 7 men to attend Bombing Course	W/m
March 24 6pm	Training in accordance with weekly programme. Lieut H. M. Lambert having been transferred to 3rd Grain A.S.C. to struck of the strength of this unit	Appendix II W/m

WAR DIARY
or
INTELLIGENCE SUMMARY.
(Erase heading not required.)

Army Form C. 2118.

Hour, Date, Place		Summary of Events and Information	Remarks and references to Appendices
Sutton Veny			
March 25	1916 6pm	Training in accordance with weekly programme	Appendix II W/pm
March 26	6pm	Service in Sutton Veny Church 9 a.m.	W/pm
March 27	6pm	Training as set out in weekly programme	Appendix III W/pm
		Court Martial (Dis. trial) for the trial of No 2190 Pte Wooton 1957 " H.M. Jones	
		took place in No 7 Camp and lasted from 11 a.m. to 3.30 p.m.	W/pm
March 28	6pm	Training in accordance with weekly programme	Apt III W/pm do W/pm
March 29	6pm	do do	
		Lieut R.C. Horan having proceeded overseas is struck off the strength of the unit	W/pm

WAR DIARY
or
INTELLIGENCE SUMMARY
(Erase heading not required.)

Army Form C. 2118.

Hour, Date, Place	Summary of Events and Information	Remarks and references to Appendices
1916 March 30 6pm	Field training in accordance with weekly programme. Capt. C. Burrows proceeded to Millbank to attend antigas lectures.	Appx III W/m W.Pro W/m W/m
March 31 6pm	Proceeding of Court hosted of Investigates Route March – Lords Hill out and back by the Seville	

W. Macworth-Macauley
Major
Commdg. 2/5 2nd London Field Ambulance

APPENDIX No. 1.

PROGRAMME OF TRAINING.

6.45 a.m.	Coffee and Biscuits.
7. 0 a.m. to 7.45 a.m.	Double 300 yds, Squad Drill Double 300 yds.
8. 0 a.m.	Breakfast.
9. 0 a.m. to 11.0 a.m.	Prepared stretchers and wagon loading drill.
11.30 a.m. to 12. 0 noon.	Physical Drill.
12.30 p.m.	Dinner.
2. 0 p.m. to 2.45 p.m.	Stretcher Drill with closed stretchers.
2.45 p.m.	Double 200 yds in fours at intervals at for 10.mins.
3. 0 p.m. to 4. 0 p.m.	Lecture or Practical First Aid.

W. Cameron Macaulay
Major
Commdg: 75th Land. Fd. Amb.

Appendix II

WEEKLY PROGRAMME OF TRAINING FOR WEEK ENDING 25.3.16.
2/5th London Field Ambulance. R.A.M.C.T.

	7.a.m. to 7.45 a.m.	9.a.m. to 12(noon).	2.p.m. to 4.p.m.
Monday.	Marching & moving in fours. Forming Section & doubling 200 yds at intervals.	Route March. (9.a.m. to 1.p.m.)	Foot, boot & Kit inspctn. (2.30 - 3.30)
Tuesday.	-do-	Squad Drill ½ hr. Physical Drill ½ hr. Practical Stretcher Drill with prepared stretcher. 1½ hour.	Lecture: 'First Aid'.
Wednesday.	-do-	Squad Drill ½ hr. Physical Drill ½ hr. Demonstration on Water disinfection or equipment. 1½ hr	Lecture. Stretcher Drill (Whistle & Signal.)
Thursday.	-do-	Field Training. (9.a.m. to 1.p.m.) Sutton Veny District.	Lecture. (2.30 - 3.30)
Friday.	-do-	Route March. (9.a.m. to 1.p.m.)	Pay.
Saturday.	-do-	Signalling 1 hr. Wagon Drill 2.hrs.	Parade for Defaulters & inefficients.
LOCALITY.	In and near Camp No.7.	Sutton Veny Dist.	In and near Camp No.7

W. Cameron Macaulay
Major. R.A.M.C.T.
Comdg: 2/5th London Field Ambnce.

No.7.Camp, Sutton Veny.
21st March 1916.

Appendix III

WEEKLY PROGRAMME OF TRAINING FOR WEEK ENDING 1.4.16.
2/5th London Field Ambulance. R.A.M.C.T.

	7.a.m. to 7.45 a.m.	9.a.m. to 12(noon).	2.p.m. to 4.p.m.
Monday.	Marching & moving in fours. Forming Section & doubling 500 yds at intervals.	Route March. (9.a.m. to 1.p.m.)	Foot, boot & Kit inspcth. 2.30 – 3.30.
Tuesday.	– do –	Squad Drill ½ hr. Physical Drill ½ hr. Demonstration Drill with prepared stretcher. 1 hour.	Lecture: Practical First Aid.
Wednesday.	– do –	Squad Drill ½ hr. Physical Drill ½ hr. Demonstration on Water Disinfection or Equipment.	Lecture. Stretcher Drill. (Whistle & Signal.)
Thursday.	– do –	Field Training. 9.a.m. to 1.p.m. Sutton Veny Dist.	Lecture. 2.30 – 3.30.
Friday.	– do –	Route March. 9.a.m. to 1.p.m.	Pay.
Saturday.	– do –	Signalling 1 hr. Wagon Drill 2 hrs.	Parade for Defaulters & inefficients.
LOCALITY.	In and near Camp.No.7.	Sutton Veny District.	In and near Camp.No.7.

W. Cansen-Macaulay
Major. R.A.M.C.T.
Commdg: 2/5th London Field Ambnce.

No.7.Camp, Sutton Veny.
25th March 1916.

Army Form C. 2118.

WAR DIARY
or
INTELLIGENCE SUMMARY.
(Erase heading not required.)

Instructions regarding War Diaries and Intelligence Summaries are contained in F. S. Regs., Part II. and the Staff Manual respectively. Title pages will be prepared in manuscript.

Hour, Date, Place	Summary of Events and Information	Remarks and references to Appendices
1916 Sutton Veny		
April 1 6pm	Training in accordance with weekly programme	Appendix I
	A case of Scabies occurred in this unit (Pte) 2328 Private E. Dalzgold of Sutton Veny Hospital	15/I/16
April 2 6pm	Church Parade at Sutton Veny Church	15/I/16
	All Blankets Shaken and aired	15/I/16
April 3 6pm	Training in accordance with weekly programme.	App I
	2190 Pte Bolton J.H. and 1989 Pte Jones N.W. sent to Detention Barracks, Wandsworth under an escort	15/I/16
April 4 6pm	Training in accordance with weekly programme in morning. Afternoon parade cancelled to enable the unit to attend funeral of Private E. Dalzgold dcd. All pallbearers & party - 8 were Shaken & aired down thereafter refilled	Appx I 15/I/16
April 5 6pm	Training in accordance with weekly programme	15/I/16
April 6 6pm	do	App I 15/I/16 do 15/I/16

WAR DIARY
INTELLIGENCE SUMMARY
(Erase heading not required.)

Army Form C. 2118.

Hour, Date, Place	Summary of Events and Information	Remarks and references to Appendices
1916 Sutton Veny April 7 8 p.m.	The whole Field Ambulance took part in a Special Tactical Exercise arranged by A.D.M.S. The scheme involved the rapid collection and evacuation of 40 wounded over difficult country and the speedy cure of a main dressing station from one points to another. The Ambulance wagons were sent to this unit for the day by the 6th & 7th Ambce & all "B" and "C" Sec^{ns}. Classes	W.T.L. W.T.L.
April 8 6 p.m.	Training in General a.n.fl. Weekly programme	App^x I W.T.L.
April 9 6 p.m.	Church parade to Sutton Veny Church. All blankets shaken and aired. A Special Saluting Salute for Transport Sectⁿ.	W.T.L.
April 10 6 p.m.	Training in accordance with weekly programme	App^x II W.T.L.
7 p.m.	Route March to Bindon Abdey & the Bowills. Kent known details to be on Rifle Range	W.T.L.

Army Form C. 2118.

WAR DIARY
~~INTELLIGENCE~~ SUMMARY.
(Erase heading not required.)

Instructions regarding War Diaries and Intelligence Summaries are contained in F.S. Regs., Part II. and the Staff Manual respectively. Title pages will be prepared in manuscript.

Hour, Date, Place	Summary of Events and Information	Remarks and references to Appendices
1916 Sutton Veny April 11 8pm	Training in accordance with weekly programme. Re inoculation commenced - 35 men inoculated today	Appx I W.G.M.
April 12 8pm	Weather bad - Training in Huts	W.G.M.
	1 N.C.O. and 40 men lent to 4th F. Amb. for General Scheme. (A.D.M.S. also 5 Amb. bicycles and 5 saddles lent to 6th F. Amb.) All weather on account of rain	W.G.M.
April 13 8pm	All day Route march to MERE + back by PERTWOOD and LORD'S HILL (22 miles). Dinner was cooked and eaten in the field	W.G.M.
April 14 6pm	Tactical exercise of A.D.M.S. this unit 1/6 Glos. acted as wounded. "attacks by 4th Fd. Amb."	W.G.M.

WAR DIARY
INTELLIGENCE SUMMARY
(Erase heading not required.)

Army Form C. 2118.

Hour, Date, Place	Summary of Events and Information	Remarks and references to Appendices
1916 Sutton Veny April 15 6 p.m.	42 men reinoculated – Interior & men's kits and necessaries – very satisfactory – Pay	W.J.M.
April 16 8 p.m.	Church Parade to Sutton Veny Church. Inspection of kits & Transport Section and General duties to men in hospital.	W.J.M.
April 17 6 p.m.	NCO and 40 men lent to 4th F.d Amb. as wounded – Five amb. a wagons and 5 S.y.m n'dnles lent to 6th F.d Amb. One Officer and 1 amb. a wagon lent to 6th F.d Amb. for duty on Rifle Range. 50 men inoculated – ~~Ordnance~~ (cancelled) Ordinary programme	W.J.M.

Army Form C. 2118.

WAR DIARY
OF
INTELLIGENCE SUMMARY.
(Erase heading not required.)

Instructions regarding War Diaries and Intelligence Summaries are contained in F.S. Regs., Part II. and the Staff Manual respectively. Title pages will be prepared in manuscript.

Hour, Date, Place		Summary of Events and Information	Remarks and references to Appendices
Sutton Veny 1916			
April 18 1916	6pm	Training in accordance with weekly programme	Appx III W.J.m Wm
April 19	6pm	do	do W.J.m
		26 inoculations and revaccinations. Major Culp reported unit W.J.m	
April 20	6pm	Training in accordance with weekly programme	W.J.m
April 21	6pm	Major Inchcombe Reported 7 days sick leave for M.R. Culp. Good Friday - Church parade Sutton Veny Church	W.J.m
April 22	6pm	Training in accordance with weekly programme	W.J.m
April 23	6pm	Church Parade Sutton Veny Church	W.J.m
April 24	6pm	Training in accordance with weekly programme	Appx III W.J.m
April 25	6pm	do	do W.J.m
		Capt. C. Burrows detailed for temporary duty as R.M.O. 1/24 Batt. L.R.	
		Lieut. B.H. Pearse having reported is attached to this unit for duty and posted to "A" Section.	W.J.m
		New pack equipment issued to all ranks.	W.J.m

Army Form C. 2118.

WAR DIARY
~~INTELLIGENCE SUMMARY.~~
(Erase heading not required.)

Instructions regarding War Diaries and Intelligence Summaries are contained in F.S. Regs., Part II. and the Staff Manual respectively. Title pages will be prepared in manuscript.

Hour, Date, Place		Summary of Events and Information	Remarks and references to Appendices
1916 Sutton Veny			
April 26	6 p.m.	Training in accordance with weekly Programme	Appx III W/M
— 27	6 p.m.	do	do W/M
		Major W.C. Macaulay returns from sick leave	W/M
— 28	6 p.m.	Training in accordance with weekly Programme	Appx III W/M
— 29	6 p.m.	The unit moved from Camp No 7 Sutton Veneton to Camp No 9	W/M
— 30	6 p.m.	Church parade to Sutton Veny Church	W/M

W. Cameron Macaulay
Major
O/C 1/5 Lond Fd Amb C Austr?

Appendix I

WEEKLY PROGRAMME OF TRAINING FOR WEEK ENDING 8.4.16.
2/5th London Field Ambulance. R.A.M.C.T.

	7.a.m. to 7.45.a.m.	9.a.m. to 12.noon.	2.p.m. to 4.p.m.
Monday.	Marching & moving in fours. Forming Section & doubling 300 yds at intervals.	Route March. 9.a.m. to 1.p.m.	Foot, Boot & Kit inspection. 2.30 - 3.30.p.m.
Tuesday.	-do-	Squad Drill ½hr. Physical Drill ½hr. Drill with prepared stretcher 1½hrs.	Lecture. Practical First Aid.
Wednesday.	-do-	Field Training. 9.a.m1 to 1.p.m.	Lecture. 2.30.p.m. to 3.30.
Thursday.	-do-	Squad Drill ½hr. Physical Drill ½hr. Demonstration on Water Disinfection or Equipment 1½hrs.	Lecture. Wagon Loading.
Friday.	-do-	Field Training. 9.a.m. to 1.p.m.	Pay.
Saturday.	-do-	Sighting 1.hr. Wagon Drill 2 hrs.	Parade for Defaulters and inefficients.
LOCALITY.	In & near Camp.No.7.	Sutton Veny Dist.	In & near Camp.7.

W. Cameron Macaulay Major

Major. R.A.M.C.T.
Commdg: 2/5th London Field Ambulance.

No.7.Camp, Sutton Veny.
25th March 1916.

Appendix II

WEEKLY PROGRAMME OF TRAINING FOR WEEK-ENDING 15.4.16.
2/5th London Field Ambulance. R.A.M.C.T.

	7.a.m. to 7.45.a.m.	9.a.m. to 12.noon.	21p.m. to 4.p.m.
Monday.	Marching & moving in fours. Forming section & doubling 300.yds at intervals.	Route March. (9.a.m. to 1.p.m.)	Foot, Boot & Kit inspection.
Tuesday.	- do -	Squad Drill ½hr. Physical Drill ½hr. Stretcher Drill with prepared stretcher 1½hrs.	Lecture. Practical First Aid.
Wednesday.	- do -	Field Training. 9.a.m. to 5.p.m. Lords Hill.	
Thursday.	- do -	Squad Drill ½hr. Physical Drill ½hr. Demonstration on water disinfection or Equipment 1½hrs.	Lecture. Wagon Loading.
Friday.	- do -	Field Training. 9.a.m. to 1.p.m. Sutton Veny & Tytherington.	Pay.
Saturday.	- do -	Signalling 1 hr. Wagon Drill. 2 hrs.	Parade for Defaulters and Inefficients.
LOCALITY.	In & near Camp.No.7.	Sutton Veny District.	In & near Camp.7.

D. Cameron Macaulay
Major. R.A.M.C.T.
Commdg: 2/5th London Field Ambulance.

No.7.Camp, Sutton Veny.
April 8th 1916.

WEEKLY PROGRAMME OF TRAINING FOR WEEK-ENDING 22.4.16.
2/5th. London field Ambulance. R.A.M.C.T.

	7.a.m. to 7.45.a.m.	9.a.m. to 12.noon.	2.p.m. to 4.p.m.
Monday.	Marching and moving in fours. Forming Section And doubling 300 yds. at intervals.	Route March. (9. a.m. to 1.p.m.)	Foot, Boot & Kit inspection. 2.30. to 3.30. pm
Tuesday.	- do -	Squad Drill ½ hr. Physical Drill ½ hr. Stretcher Drill with prepared stretcher 1½ hrs.	Lecture. Practical First Aid.
Wednesday.	- do -	Field Training. (With exception of one Section engaged in Brigade Operations.) (9. a.m. to 1. p.m.)	Lecture. (2.30. to 3.30)
Thursday.	- do -	Squad Drill ½ hr. Physical Drill ½ hr. Demonstration on Water Disinfection of Equipment. 1½ hrs.	Lecture. Wagon Loading.
Friday.	- do -	Field Training. 9.a.m. to 1.p.m. Sutton Veny and Tytherington.	Pay.
Saturday.	- do -	Signalling. 1.hr. Wagon Drill 2.hrs.	Parade for Defaulters & inefficients.
LOCALITY.	In & near Camp No.7.	Sutton Veny District.	In & near Camp No. 7.

W. Cameron Macaulay
Major
Av Major. R.A.M.C.T.
Commndg. 2/5th. London Field Ambulance.

No. 7. Camp, Sutton Veny.
15th. April 1916.

Appendix IV

WEEKLY PROGRAMME OF TRAINING FOR WEEK-ENDING 29.4.16.
2/5th London Field Ambulance. R.A.M.C.T.

	7.a.m. to 7.45.a.m.	9.a.m. to 12.noon.	2.p.m. to 4.p.m.
Monday.	Squad Drill and Doubling, if wet Physical Drill in hut.	Route March. 9.a.m. to 1.p.m.	Foot, Boot and Kit inspection. 2.30 to 3.30.p.m.
Tuesday.	- do -	Demonstration or Lecture by Section Officers 1.hr. Stretcher Drill by whistle and signal. Whiten Hill. 10.15 - 12.15.p.m.	Wagon Loading. 2.p.m. to 3.p.m. First Aid. 3.p.m. to 4.p.m.
Wednesday.	- do -	Field Training. Cotley Hill. 9.a.m. to 12.30 p.m.	Demonstration on Equipment. 2 - 3. First Aid. 3 - 4.
Thursday.	- do -	Demonstration or Lecture by Section Officers.1.hr. Company Drill. Whiten Hill. 10.15.a.m. to 12.15.p.m.	Wagon Loading. 2.p.m. to 3.p.m. First Aid. 3.p.m. to 4.p.m.
Friday.	- do -	Field Training. Shear Water. 9.a.m. to 1.p.m.	Pay. 2.30.p.m.
Saturday.	- do -	Wagon Drill. 2.hrs. Signalling. 1.hr.	Parade for Defaulters and Inefficients.
LOCALITY.	In & near Camp.7.	Sutton Veny District.	In & near Camp.7.

W. James W. Macaulay
Major. R.A.M.C.T.
Commdg: 2/5th London Field Ambulance.

No.7.Camp, Sutton Veny.
22nd April 1916.

Army Form C. 2118.

WAR DIARY
INTELLIGENCE SUMMARY.
(Erase heading not required.)

Instructions regarding War Diaries and Intelligence Summaries are contained in F.S. Regs., Part II. and the Staff Manual respectively. Title pages will be prepared in manuscript.

Hour, Date, Place		Summary of Events and Information	Remarks and references to Appendices
1916 Sutton Veny			
May 1	6 pm	Training in accordance with weekly programme. Major W.T. Macaulay proceeded from A Sect. to C Sect. to B Sect. - C - B.	Appx I WJM WJM
May 2	6 pm	20 Reg. Stretcher Bearers per Batt. 160 + hy. Bda. at this unit for training in stretcher drill & first aid daily 5th further orders.	WJM Appx I WJM do WJM do WJM
May 3	6 pm	Training in accordance with weekly programme do	do WJM
May 4	6 pm	do	do WJM
May 5	6 pm	do	do WJM
May 6	6 pm	do	WJM
May 7	6/9 pm	Week end leave suspended throughout D.S. Church Parade Sutton Veny Church 9.15 am	WJM

Army Form C. 2118.

WAR DIARY
or
INTELLIGENCE SUMMARY.
(Erase heading not required.)

Instructions regarding War Diaries and Intelligence
Summaries are contained in F. S. Regs., Part II.
and the Staff Manual respectively. Title pages
will be prepared in manuscript.

Hour, Date, Place	Summary of Events and Information	Remarks and references to Appendices
1916 Sutton Veney May 8 6 p.m.	It has rained heavy all day necessitating dull lectures in huts	W.J.M.
May 9 6 p.m.	Route march of 180th R of 15 to in street this unit took part (6 off. 102 rank & file 3 amb. wagons & cookcart)	W.J.M. App.I W.J.M. do W.J.M.
May 10 6 p.m.	Training in accordance with weekly Programme	
May 11 6 p.m.	do	
May 12 6 p.m.	Major R. Corfe detailed on D.S. duties to attend Gas Course at Rollestone May 12th-13th ADMS meets off. on J.A. to-day in recent happenings in Barrowwist Divn. Training in accordance with weekly Programme	W.J.M. W.J.M. App.II W.J.M. do
May 13 6 p.m.	do	do W.J.M.
May 14 6 p.m.	do	
May 15	Church Parade Sutton Veney Church	

WAR DIARY / INTELLIGENCE SUMMARY

Army Form C. 2118.

Hour, Date, Place		Summary of Events and Information	Remarks and references to Appendices
1916 Sutton Veny			
May 15	8pm	Route March	Appx II 6/JW
May 16	6pm	Training in accordance with week's programme	do 6/JW
May 17	6pm	do	
May 18	6pm	do	do 6/JW
May 19	6pm	do	
May 20	6pm	Church Parade to S. John Veny Church at 9.45am all clocks put forward to 3.9am	6/JW Appx IV 6/JW
May 21	6pm	Route March in accordance with week's programme	do 6/JW
May 22	6pm	do	
May 23	6pm	Capt. G.H.R. Wade F.R.C.S. having reported for duty is taken on the Strength as from today and is posted to "B" Section	6/JW
May 24	6pm	Divisional Route March — CROCKERTON GREEN — LONGLEAT PARK — NEWBURY — LONGBRIDGE DEVERILL.	6/JW

Army Form C. 2118.

WAR DIARY
or
INTELLIGENCE SUMMARY.
(Erase heading not required.)

Instructions regarding War Diaries and Intelligence Summaries are contained in F. S. Regs., Part II. and the Staff Manual respectively. Title pages will be prepared in manuscript.

Hour, Date, Place		Summary of Events and Information	Remarks and references to Appendices
1916 Sutton Veny			
May 25	1916 6pm	Training in accordance with weekly Programme	App II 13/hr
May 26	6pm	The unit took part in a Divisional Attack	App I 13/hr
May 27	6pm	Training in accordance with weekly Programme	App IV 13/hr
May 28	6pm	Church Parade to Sutton Veny Church	13/hr
May 29	6pm	Route March (UPTON SCUDAMORE)	13/hr
May 30	6pm	Rehearsal N. of SCRATCHBURY HILL for Review by H.M. the King	13/hr
May 31	6pm	H.M. the King reviewed the 60(Lond) Div" on ground N of SCRATCHBURY HILL	13/hr

W. Cameron Macaulay
Lt Col
I/O.C. 2/5 Ld Field Amb"

Appendix I

PROGRAMME OF TRAINING FOR WEEK ENDING 7.5.16.
2/5th London Field Ambulance. R.A.M.C.T.

	7.a.m. to 7.45.a.m.	9.a.m. to 12.30.p.m.	2.p.m. to 4.p.m.
Monday.	Movements in fours. and doubling.	Route March. (Marching Order.)	Equipment, Foot Boot, and Kit inspection.
Tuesday.	Squad Drill.	Demonstration or Lecture. Stretcher Drill. (Whiten Hill).	Loading Technical vehicles. First Aid.
Wednesday.	Movements in fours. and doubling.	Field Training. (Crokerton Green & Long Leat Wood).	Improvisation. First Aid.
Thursday.	Squad Drill.	Demonstration or Lecture. Company Drill. (Whiten Hill).	Equipment. First Aid.
Friday.	Movements in fours and doubling.	Field Training. (Scratchbury Hill.)	Pay.
Saturday.	Squad Drill.	Wagon Drill. 2 hrs. Semaphore Signalling.	Defaulters Drill.
	Physical Drill every afternoon except Saturday, for employed staff (Cooks, Orderlies in Q.M.Stores, Orderly Room, etc.,) under the Orderly Sergeant from 2.p.m. to 2.30.p.m.)		
LOCALITY.	In & near Camp.9.		In & near Camp.9.

W. Cameron Macaulay
Major

Major. R.A.M.C.T.
Commdg: 2/5th London Field Ambulance.

No.9.Camp, Sutton Veny.
30th April 1916.

Appendix II

PROGRAMME OF TRAINING FOR WEEK-ENDING 14.5.16.
2/5th London Field Ambulance. R.A.M.C.T.

	7.a.m. to 7.45.a.m.	9.a.m. to 12.30.p.m.	2.p.m. to 4.p.m.
Monday.	Movements in fours and doubling.	Route March. (Marching Order).	Equipment. Foot, Boot and Kit inspection.
Tuesday.	Squad Drill.	Demonstration or Lecture Stretcher Drill. (Whiten Hill).	Loading Technical vehicles. First Aid.
Wednesday.	Movements in fours and doubling.	Field Training. (Scratchbury Hill).	Sanitation on the Line of March and in temp'y Camps. First Aid.
Thursday.	Squad Drill.	Demonstration or Lecture Company Drill. (Whiten Hill).	Equipment. First Aid.
Friday.	Movements in fours and doubling.	Field Training. (Tytherington Hill)	Pay.
Saturday.	Squad Drill.	Wagon Drill. 2.hrs. Semaphore Signalling.	Defaulters Drill.

Physical Drill every afternoon except Saturday for employed staff (Cooks, Orderlies in Q.M.Stores, Orderly Room, etc.,) under the Orderly Sergeant, from 2.p.m. to 2.30.p.m.)

LOCALITY. In & near Camp.9.   In & near Camp.9.

Major. R.A.M.C.T.
Commdg: 2/5th London Field Ambulance.

No.9.Camp, Sutton Veny.
6th May 1916.

Appendix III

PROGRAMME OF TRAINING FOR WEEK-ENDING 21.5.16.
2/5th London Field Ambulance. R.A.M.C.T.

	7.a.m. to 7.45.a.m.	9.a.m. to 12.30.p.m.	2.p.m. to 4.p.m.
Monday.	Movements in fours and doubling.	Route March. (Marching Order).	Equipment. Foot, Boot and Kit inspection.
Tuesday.	Squad Drill.	Demonstration or Lecture Stretcher Drill. (Whiten Hill).	Loading technical vehicles. First Aid.
Wednesday.	Movements in fours and doubling.	Field Training. (Shear Water).	Military Hygiene. First Aid.
Thursday.	Squad Drill.	Demonstration or Lecture Company Drill. (Whiten Hill).	Equipment. First Aid.
Friday.	Movements in fours and doubling.	Field Training. (Cotley Hill).	Pay.
Saturday.	Squad Drill.	Wagon Drill. 2.hrs. Semaphore Signalling.	Defaulters Drill.

Physical Drill every afternoon except Saturday for employed staff (Cooks, Orderlies, in Q.M.Stores, Orderly Room etc,₩) under the Orderly Sergeant from 2.p.m. to 2.30.p.m.)

LOCALITY. In & Near Camp.9/ In & near Camp.9.

W. Cameron Macaulay
Major

Major. R.A.M.C.T.
Commdg: 2/5th London Field Ambulance.

No.9.Camp, Sutton Veny.
13th May 1916.

Appendix IV

2/5TH LONDON FIELD AMBULANCE
PROGRAMME OF TRAINING FOR WEEK-ENDING 28 - 5.- 16.

	7.a.m. to 7.45.a.m.	9.a.m. to 12./30.p.m.	2.p.m. to 4.p.m.
MONDAY	Movements in fours & Doubling	Field Training. (Tytherington Hill)	Equipment Foot Boot & Kit Inspection
TUESDAY	Squad Drill	Lecture on "Sanitation on the March & in the Field	Loading Technical Vehicles First Aid.
WEDNESDAY.	D I V I S I O N A L R O U T E M A R C H		
THURSDAY.	Squad Drill	Lecture on "Sanitation in Barracks & Billets.	Equipment First Aid
FRIDAY.	D I V I S I O N A L A T T A C K.		
SATURDAY	Squad Drill	Wagon Drill.(2 Hrs) Semaphore Signalling.	Defaulters Drill

Physical Drill every afternoon except Saturay for employed Staff (Cooks, Orderlies in Q.M% Stores, Orderly Room, etc:.) under the Orderly Sergeant, from 2.0.p.m. to 2. 30.p.m.

LOCALITY   In and near Camp No. 9.   In & near Camp No.9

W. Cameron Macaulay
Major

SUTTON VENY,
May 20th 1916.
                        Major. R.A.M.C.T.
            Commanding 2/5th London Field Ambulance.

Appendix V

60th DIVISIONAL EXERCISE – 26th MAY 1916.

1. The Division deploying for Attack.

2. A Frontal Attack combined with a Flank attack.

SITUATION.

Ref: 1" O.S. Sheets 122 and 123.

A Raiding Force, of which the 3rd Corps (comprising the 60th and 61st Divisions) forms a part, has landed on the South Coast and is moving northwards. The enemy is hastily sending troops Southwards to meet invaders. His aeroplanes were over Gillingham on the 25th May.

The 3rd Corps has been pushed on in advance to seize the junction at Westbury; and on the night of the 25/26th May has reached the L.&.S.W.Rly.- the 60th Division about Semley and the 61st Division about Gillingham.

At 6.a.m. 26th May, the G.O.C. 60th Div, receives the following message: -

"60. Div.
G.51.   twentysixth   AAA.
Enemy reliably reported to be holding high ground on both sides of the main East Knoyle - Westbury Road, about 4 miles South of Warminster with a weak Div AAA Hostile reinforcements are expected to reach that position by 1.p.m. to-day detraining at Warminster AAA 60th Div. will attack enemy East of the road (exclusive) AAA 61st Div. will attack West of road (inclusive) AAA. Divisional Mounted Troops must endeavour to locate flanks of enemy position as early as possible AAA. Attacks to commence at 11.a.m. at which hour leading attacking troops should cross the line Chicklade - Kilmington AAA Every endeavour is to be made to drive the enemy Westwards AAA Corps Orders follow AAA. Acknowledge.
            Third Corps.
            5 a.m. "

On receipt of this message, the G.O.C., 60th Div. issues orders for the move to the places of assembly prior to the attack on the enemy.

2/5th London Field Ambulance

June 1916

60 u. Ons

COMMITTEE FOR THE MEDICAL HISTORY OF THE WAR
Date 19 OCT. 1916

WAR DIARY or INTELLIGENCE SUMMARY

(Erase heading not required.)

Army Form C. 2118

Place	Date	Hour	Summary of Events and Information	Remarks and references to Appendices
Sutton Veny	1916 June 1	8pm	Embarkation leave starts this morning - 30% all ranks on leave for 4 days	19/m
	2		Training in accordance with weekly programme of Training	app I as 19/m
	3		do	do 19/m
SUTTON VENY, WILTS	4		Church Parade Sutton Veny Church	19/m
	5		Training in accordance with weekly training programme	App II 19/m
	6		do	do
	7		do	do 19/m
	8		Rev G. H. Fendick C.F. attached to this unit for rations pillot	19/m
			Training in accordance with weekly programme	App III
			Capt L.L. Preston and Capt L. Melton report for duty and are taken on strength of this unit	19/m
	9		Training in accordance with weekly programme	App II
			Capt E. Crescent & Capt J.H. Jackman C.F. attached to the unit for rations & billets	

WAR DIARY
or
INTELLIGENCE SUMMARY

(Erase heading not required.)

Army Form C. 2118

Instructions regarding War Diaries and Intelligence Summaries are contained in F.S. Regs., Part II. and the Staff Manual respectively. Title Pages will be prepared in manuscript.

Place	Date	Hour	Summary of Events and Information	Remarks and references to Appendices
Sutton Veny	1916 June 10	6pm	Training in accordance with weekly programme	Appx II within
	11	"	do	within
	12	"	do	Appx III
			Capt. L. Walton transferred to 4th Lond. Fd. Amb & taken off the strength of the unit	within
			Capt. Clarke " from " " " "	within
	13		Training in accordance with weekly programme	Appx III within
			do	
SUTTON VENY.	14		Secret orders for Embarkation of Division received	within
WILTS	15		Parade of Officers, men & transport for inspection as to fitness for proceeding overseas	within
	16		Boards of Survey held on clothing. Apps of units & war Personal Private property of Officers taken (list for insurance) sent over	within
	17		Reserve hospital stores returned to D.O. Barracks.	within
	18		Inspection of hutments & futures with requisitions & D.O.R.E	within
	19		Stray tools, fatigue parties returned to D.O.R.E from barn	within

WAR DIARY or INTELLIGENCE SUMMARY

Army Form C. 2118

(Erase heading not required.)

Instructions regarding War Diaries and Intelligence Summaries are contained in F.S. Regs., Part II. and the Staff Manual respectively. Title Pages will be prepared in manuscript.

Place	Date	Hour	Summary of Events and Information	Remarks and references to Appendices
SUTTON VENY, WILTS	1916 June 20	6pm	Patrol pockets sewn in tunics for overseas. Habiliments scrubbed over with grease. Rubbish burnt.	
	21		Gas helmets, goggles, First Field Dressings, identity discs re-inspected. Blankets, bed boards, trestles, tables &c. returned to O.O. Stores &c.	
	22		Unit travelled by train to Southampton and embarked as follows:- On S.S. INVENTOR 3 off, 1 Chaplain 68 other ranks 18 Vehicles 2 bicycles 54 horses On S.S. CONNAUGHT 7 off + 156 other ranks	
	23		Disembark at HAVRE & proceed by route march to Rest Camp Nº 2 (tents) near SANVIC	
LE HAVRE	24		Route march to gare maritime LE HAVRE & entrain. Two draught horses chosen to complete establishment.	
	25		Arrive ST POL via ROUEN, AMIENS & ABBÉVILLE. Route march to HÉRICOURT to close billets	
HÉRICOURT	26		Two NCOs and 10 men A.S.C., M.T. taken on strength as attached with 7 motor ambulance wagons (5 TALBOTS and 2 FORDS) and 2 motor bicycles (1 DOUGLAS & 1 TRIUMPH)	

WAR DIARY or INTELLIGENCE SUMMARY

Army Form C. 2118

Place	Date	Hour	Summary of Events and Information	Remarks and references to Appendices
HÉRICOURT	June 27 1916	6pm	Capt. L. L. PRESTON, 1 N.C.O. & 8 men temporarily attached to 42nd C.C.S at AUBIGNY by order of A.D.M.S. Unit by route march reaches PÉNIN & goes into close billets	W/D
PÉNIN	28	8pm	Capt. F. St. J. STEADMAN, Capt. B. CLARKE and personnel of "B" section 1 lumber wagon and 1 water cart proceed to HAUTE-AVESNES for temporary attachment to 1/3 Highland Field Amb= until July 6 by order of A.D.M.S. Capt. G. L. WHALE left to report for duty to No 13 General Hospital BOULOGNE by order of A.D.M.S. and is taken off the strength of this unit. The A.D.M.S notifies that he is applying for a reinforcement to replace Capt. WHALE. A reception hospital has been established in the village by this unit for the sick to of the 180th Inf. Bde.	
	29	6pm	Lieut F. J. MORRIN has been detailed to attend sick to of O.B. AMM. COL. at LABELLE ÉPINE daily commencing today by order of A.D.M.S.	W/D

WAR DIARY
or
INTELLIGENCE SUMMARY

Army Form C. 2118

Instructions regarding War Diaries and Intelligence Summaries are contained in F.S. Regs, Part II. and the Staff Manual respectively. Title Pages will be prepared in manuscript.

(Erase heading not required.)

Place	Date	Hour	Summary of Events and Information	Remarks and references to Appendices
PÉNIN	1916 June 29	6pm	Letter received from General Headquarters O/B/1658 dated 27/6/16 stating that War Establishment Part VII will be adhered to by all Divisions serving in FRANCE except those which belong to military forces of self governing Dominions.	WJW
			4010. BALVER attached to unit as Interpreter under direction of O.C. French Mission to D.S.	WJW
	30	8pm	Three privates (2 from 2/17 Bn L.R. and 1 from 4/6 Bn L.R.) attached to unit as stretcher bearers attached.	WJW
			Telephone message received 8pm from Asst. ordering the unit to proceed to rest quarters at TINQUETTE bivouac	WJW

R.C. Rose
MAJOR R.A.M.C., T.
COMMANDING 2/5th LONDON FIELD AMBULANCE.

Appendix I

PROGRAMME OF TRAINING FOR WEEK-ENDING 4.6.15.
2/5th London Field Ambulance. R.A.M.C.T.

	7.a.m. to 7.45.a.m.	9.a.m. to 12.30.p.m.	2.p.m. to 4.p.m.
Monday.	Movements in fours and doubling.	Route March.	Equipment. Foot, Boot & Kit inspection.
Tuesday.	Squad Drill.	Stretcher Drill. Lecture on Sanitation in Barracks & Billets.	Loading Technical vehicles. First Aid.
Wednesday.	–	Inspection by H.M. the King.	–
Thursday.	Squad Drill.	Company Drill. Lecture or Company Drill.	Equipment. First Aid.
Friday.	Movements in fours and doubling.	Route March.	First Aid. Pay.
Saturday.	Squad Drill.	Wagon Drill. 2hrs. Lecture or Demonstration.	Defaulters Drill.

Physical Drill every afternoon except Saturday for employed Staff (Cooks, Orderlies in Q.M.Stores, Orderly Room.etc.,) under the Orderly Sergeant from 2.p.m. to 2.30.p.m.

LOCALITY. In & near Camp.9.   In & near Camp.9.

Major. R.A.M.C.T.
Commdg: 2/5th London Field Ambulance.

No.9.Camp, Sutton Veny.
27th May 1916.

Appendix II

PROGRAMME OF TRAINING FOR WEEK-ENDING 2.6.16.
2/5th London Field Ambulance. R.A.M.C.T.

	7.a.m. to 7.45.a.m.	9.a.m. to 12.30.p.m.	2.p.m. to 4.p.m.
Monday.	Physical Drill.	Route March.	Equipment, Foot, Boot & Kit inspection.
Tuesday.	Squad Drill.	Stretcher Drill. Lecture on Geneva Convention.	Loads of vehicles. First Aid.
Wednesday.	Physical Drill.	Field Training. Lord's Hill.	First Aid.
Thursday.	Squad Drill.	Company Drill. Lecture or Demonstration.	First Aid. Pay. Equipment.
Friday.	Physical Drill.	Route March.	First Aid. Pay.
Saturday.	Squad Drill.	Wagon Drill. 1½ hrs. Lecture or Demonstration.	Defaulters Drill.

Physical Drill every afternoon except Saturday for employed Staff (Cooks, Orderlies in Q.M.Stores, Orderly Room etc.,) under the Orderly Sergeant from 2.p.m. to 2.30.p.m.

LOCALITY. In & near Camp.9. In & near Camp.9.

Major R.A.M.C.T.
Commdg: 2/5th London Field Ambulance.

No.9.Camp, Sutton Veny.
2nd June 1916.

Appendix III

PROGRAMME OF TRAINING FOR WEEK ENDING 17.6.1916.
2/5th. London Field Ambulance, R.A.M.C.T.

	7 a.m. to 7.45 a.m.	9 a.m. to 12.30 p.m.	2 p.m. to 4 p.m.
Monday.	Squad Drill.	Route March	Equipment, Foot Boot and Kit Inspection.
Tuesday.	Physical Drill	Stretcher Drill. Lecture on Military Hygiene.	Loads of Vehicles. First Aid.
Wednesday.	Squad Drill.	Field Training. Whiten Hill.	First Aid.
Thursday.	Physical Drill.	Company Drill. Lecture or Demonstration.	First Aid. Equipment.
Friday.	Squad Drill.	Route March.	First Aid. Pay.
Saturday.	Physical Drill.	Wagon Drill 1½ hrs. Lecture or Demonstration.	Defaulters' Drill.

Physical Drill every afternoon except Saturday for employed staff (Cooks, Orderlies in Q.M.S., Orderly Room Clerks etc.) under Orderly Sergeant from 2 p.m. to 2.30 p.m.

Locality. In and near Camp No.9.   In and near Camp No.9.

[signature]
Major
for Major R.A.M.C.
for Major commndg. 2/5th. London Field Ambulance.

Camp No.9.
Sutton Veny.
June 10th. 1916.

PROGRAMME OF TRAINING FOR WEEK ENDING 26/4/16

MEDICAL.

Vol II

Confidential

War Diary
— of —
2/5th London Field Ambulance

From July 1st 1916. To July 31st 1916.

MEDICAL.
Army Form C. 2118

WAR DIARY
INTELLIGENCE SUMMARY
(Erase heading not required.)

Instructions regarding War Diaries and Intelligence Summaries are contained in F.S. Regs, Part II. and the Staff Manual respectively. Title Pages will be prepared in manuscript.

Place	Date	Hour	Summary of Events and Information	Remarks and references to Appendices
PERNN.	1916 July 1st	9 a.m.	In accordance with orders received late last evening, this unit is moving this evening to Tinques as TINQUETTE.	R.C.
		2 p.m.	The move has been carried, accommodation is very crowded & bad.	R.C.
TINQUETTE	July 2nd	9.45 a.m.	Church Parade in one of the huts. The new camp is very low lying, receives all the drainage from a neighbouring camp, & sanitation is difficult, the soil is clay too. A reception Hospital for surrounding units has been established.	R.C.
	July 3rd	10 a.m.	Staff Sergt. Gillard has been granted 7 days leave to England by the G.O.C. in consequence of dangerous illness of his wife.	R.C.
	July 4th	10 a.m.	A party, consisting of 2 Sergts., 2 Corpls. & 8 men has been detailed, in accordance with orders received, to carry out the works of tapping men of this Division at TINQUES under the supervision of an A.S.C. Officer.	R.C.
	July 5th	6 p.m.	"C" Section under Major MACAULAY & Capt. BROCKMAN has been sent up to 2/1st Highland Field Ambulance at HAUTE AVESNES for instructional purposes until July 9th. "B" Section has to-day returned from 1/3rd Highland Fd. Amb. to the unit for duty.	R.C.

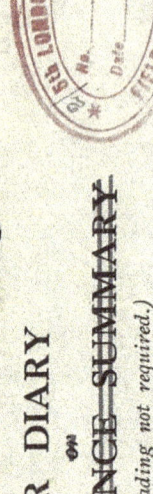

Army Form C. 2118

WAR DIARY
~~INTELLIGENCE SUMMARY~~
(Erase heading not required.)

Instructions regarding War Diaries and Intelligence Summaries are contained in F. S. Regs., Part II. and the Staff Manual respectively. Title Pages will be prepared in manuscript.

Place	Date	Hour	Summary of Events and Information	Remarks and references to Appendices
TINQUETTE	July 6	9 a.m.	Sanitary & drainage is very bad in this Camp, & the unit is to a great extent employed in improving matters - Promotions of NCOs & men have been made to complete establishment -	R.C.
	July 8	9 a.m.		R.C.
	July 9	9.10 a.m.	"A" Section under Capt. BURROWS & Lieut. MORRIN has this morning been sent up to ECOIVRES, to be attached to the 1/2nd Highland Field Ambulance for instructional purposes until July 13th inst. -	
		9 p.m.	"C" Section has this evening returned to the unit from HAUTE AVESNES.	R.C.
	July 10	2 p.m.	Capt. L.W. HOWLETT has to-day reported for duty with this unit -	R.C.
	July 12	6 p.m.	An advance party under Capt. DRAKE-BROCKMAN proceeded to HAUTE AVESNES, the 1/3rd (H'fd) Field Amb - proceeding to TINQUETTE to relieve advance party of 1/3rd (H'fd) Field Amb -	W/m
HAUTE - AVESNES	July 13	6 p.m.	Capt. CLARKE with nursing orderlies proceeded in motor ambulance at 8.30 p.m. to HAUTE-AVESNES to take over Dst. Rest Station vacated by 1/3rd (H'fd) Fd. Amb. Remainder of unit proceeded by route march tr.nr station at HAUTE - AVESNES to form a Dst Rest Staton.	
			"A" Section under Capt. C. BURROWS and Lieut. F. J. MORRIN rejoins unit at HAUTE - AVESNES	W/m

WAR DIARY
INTELLIGENCE SUMMARY

(Erase heading not required.)

Army Form C. 2118

Place	Date	Hour	Summary of Events and Information	Remarks and references to Appendices
HAUTE - AVESNES	1916 July 14	6pm	The unit is settling down to its new work. The Div. Rest Station has been taken over and is in working order. The following Army Troops are attached to the unit for Ra. Returns and discipline as from today:— 113616 Cpl. R. SMITH 1st Prov. Co. R.E. 5956 Pte. T. SCANLAN 2nd Bn. Manchester Regt. 130851 Pionr. A. EMMOTT No 4 Sect., R.E. 1876 Pte. S. HANSELL 23rd Bn. Royl Fusiliers 14990 Pte. J. CROWLEY 8th Bn. Irish Fusiliers 3148 Pte. J. GRIEG 3/7th Bn. Royal Highlanders 105004 Spr. W. GUINNESS 230th A.T. Coy. R.E.	W/In
	16	6pm	Q-M Serg. C. GILLARD has returned from leave.	W/In
	23	3pm	Church Parade in the Theatre	W/In

WAR DIARY or INTELLIGENCE SUMMARY

Army Form C. 2118

Place	Date	Hour	Summary of Events and Information	Remarks and references to Appendices
HAUTE-AVESNES	July 1916 26	8 pm	The unit was visited and inspected by G.O.C. 60th Lond. Dist.	WJm
	27	8 pm	Capt. L.N. HOWLETT has been detailed to attend the sick at wagon lines of the 50th Corps Artillery at 9 a.m. daily at BOIS D'HABARCQ until further notice.	WJm
			No 1952 Pte A. CARTER and No 2284 Pte H.S. HAWES have been detailed as orderlies to the Convalescent Company, HERMAVILLE. The late he attached to that company for Pay, Rations and Discipline.	WJm
	28	8 pm	Lieut F.J. MORRIN is detailed to attend Conference on Gas Poisoning at the Army Anti-Gas School ST. POL. The conference will last from July 29 to Aug. 2, 1916.	
			The following men having been evacuated sick are struck off the strength:-	
			2745 Dvr. PARKER, F.C. as from 1/7/16	
			2136 Pte BUTCHER, J " " 8/7/16.	
			Authority III'd Army Eve. Memo. No 18.	WJm

WAR DIARY

INTELLIGENCE SUMMARY

Army Form C. 2118

Place	Date	Hour	Summary of Events and Information	Remarks and references to Appendices
HAUTE-AVESNES	1916 July 28	6pm	Capt. C. BURROWS of this unit is sick in Hospital at No 42 Casualty Clearing Station AUBIGNY as from yesterday	
	29	6pm	The D.M.S. III-rd Army, the D.D.M.S. 17th Corps and the A.D.M.S. 60th Lond. Divt. visited Hospitals this unit.	
	31	10pm	1 N.C.O. and 7 men proceeded from this unit for duty with the 42nd Casualty Clearing Station AUBIGNY to replace 1 N.C.O. and 7 men returning to-day.	
			27485 Driver Parker having returned from a Course in Cookery on the Strength of this unit as a reinforcement authority D.M.S. III Army.	

R. Rose
MAJOR R.A.M.C. T.
COMMANDING 2/5th LONDON FIELD AMBULANCE

MEDICAL

Confidential

Aug. 1916.

Vol 3

War. Diary.
- of -
2/5th London. Field. Ambulance.

From August. 1st. 1916. to. August. 31st. 1916.

COMMITTEE FOR THE
MEDICAL HISTORY OF THE WAR
Date -5 OCT. 1916

Original.

WAR DIARY

INTELLIGENCE SUMMARY

Army Form C. 2118
MEDICAL
SHEET I

Place	Date 1916	Hour	Summary of Events and Information	Remarks and references to Appendices
HAUTE-AVESNES	Aug. 3	6pm	M2/163285 Private M.J. DIGNUM (60th Divl. Supply Column) having reported for duty is taken on the strength of A.S.C., M.T. attached from this date. Lieut. L.J. Morris returned to duty his Gas Sentence at St. POL.	WJM WJM
	4.	6pm	Col. GRAY, C.B., Consulting Surgeon 3rd Army with D.D.M.S. 17th Corps and A.D.M.S. 60th (Lond) Divn. visited the Hospital and discussed the subject of evacuation &c. of special classes of casualties.	WJM
	5.		2735 Farrier Corpl. W. GRIMLEY, A.S.C. (attached) having been evacuated sick from the Divisional area is struck off the strength dated 5.8.16 Authority 3rd Army Circ. Memo. No 18.	WJM
			2724 Sgt. D. SMITH and 2754 Dvr. F.C. PARKER A.S.C. (attached) having been transferred to the H.T. Depot HAVRE are struck off the strength dated 4.8.16 — Authority A.G. Base CR/26397C dated 15.5.16	WJM
			Pte H.R. HIGGINS having been transferred from the 1st Lond. Sanitary Co. R.A.M.C. T. is taken on the strength accordingly dated 4.8.16 Authority R.A.M.C. Section Base No 1458 dated 31.7.16	WJM

WAR DIARY or INTELLIGENCE SUMMARY

Army Form C. 2118

SHEET II

Place	Date	Hour	Summary of Events and Information	Remarks and references to Appendices
HAUTE-AVESNES	1916 Aug 10	6pm	Lecture by Lieut. F.J. MORRIN on Gas poisoning founded on notes taken by him at the Conference held at 3rd Army Anti-Gas School ST POL July 29 & Aug 2nd	LS/hn
	11	8pm	Extract from List No. 94 "Appointments and Commissions" as approved by G.O.C in C. British Army in the Field :— "2/5 London Field Ambulance Major R. CORFE to be Lieut. Colonel while commanding the unit" dates June 22nd 1916.	LS/hn
	12	6pm	Meeting of Medical Officers at No. 30 Casualty Clearing Station at AUBIGNY. Col. H.M.GRAY, C.B. Consulting Surgeon 3rd Army discussed (a.d describes the application of) certain kinds of splints. W.W. Sergt ALLGROVE and 8 other ranks temporarily attached 42. C.C.S. having returned, resume their sections for S/5.	LS/hn LS/hn
	13	8pm	Church Parade in the Empire Theatre -	LS/hn
	16	6pm	Corpl. ANDREWS has left to attend a course at the Divisional Anti Gas School at FREVIN CAPELLE from Aug 17-19 inclusive	LS/hn
	19	8pm	Capt. C. BURROWS has returned from hospital to duty	LS/hn

Army Form C.2118

SHEET III

WAR DIARY
or
INTELLIGENCE SUMMARY
(Erase heading not required.)

Instructions regarding War Diaries and Intelligence Summaries are contained in F.S. Regs., Part II. and the Staff Manual respectively. Title Pages will be prepared in manuscript.

Place	Date 1916	Hour	Summary of Events and Information	Remarks and references to Appendices
HAUTE-AVESNES	Aug 19	6pm	1969 Pte A. FRENCHUM evacuated sick from the Divisional Area and struck off the strength as from 13.8.16 [Author: IIIrd Army Rve Memo No 87 Corpl. GURNEY has left to attend a course at the Divt. Antigas School at FREVIN CAPELLE from Aug 20-22 inclusive	WJn WJn
	20	6pm	Church Parade at Enquin Theatre (C of E)	WJn
	22	6pm	The undermentioned men cease to be attached to this unit as from today under instructions of 60th Divt. R.O. 806 and are attached to own majors Staff for Pay, Rations, Discipline and Billeting:- 1876 Pte HANSELL 23rd Battn R. Fus. 19990 " CROWLEY 8th " Innt Fus.	WJn
	23	6pm	The following men have been advanced from 2nd Class Clerks to 1st Class Clerks with 3rd Rate R.A.M.C. Corps Pay with effect as from 19th inst :- 1991 Pte LOWINGS, H.J. } Author, W.O. Letr. No 9/Mas/5770 1723 " BRIDGER, J.W. } (A.M.D.1) 16.12.15 1650 " FURLONG, R.V.	WJn
	23	6pm	L/Cpl HOPKINS has left to attend a course at the Divt. Anti-Gas School at FREVIN CAPELLE from Aug 24-26 inclusive	WJn

Army Form C. 2118

SHEET IV

WAR DIARY
or
INTELLIGENCE SUMMARY
(Erase heading not required.)

Place	Date 1916	Hour	Summary of Events and Information	Remarks and references to Appendices
HAUTE-AVESNES	Aug 24	6pm	Secret news M/3/75 re Gas Attacks received from ADMS intimating that a M.O. be nominated and running Orderlies be trained for dealing with cases of Gas Poisoning. This memo is based on "Memorandum on Gas Poisoning in Warfare" (S.S. 452) by D.G.M.S. Printed Armies in France. Surgeon General Burtchaell DMS 3rd Army auspices the Hospital Capt. C. BURROWS and 11 men attaches 57/4/16 Lond. Amb.ce for 7 days commencing today. Sergt. BOURNE and 11 other ranks are attaches to 54 Lond. Amb.ce for 16 days commencing 23/8/16 Lieut. F. J. MORRIN R.A.M.C. T.C. having been transferred to the M.T. Cadre for duty with the 184th and 258th Tunnelling Coys. R.E. is struck off list strength of this unit as from today. (Auth.t ADMS letter M/690 dated 23.8.16) Driver W. H. TOMLINSON, A.S.C., M.T. attaches has been granted Special leave from 22nd to the 28th inst. (Auth.t XVII Corps letter A.Q./557 21.8.16)	W/Jm W/Jm W/Jm W/Jm W/Jm W/Jm

Army Form C. 2118.

SHEET V.

WAR DIARY
or
INTELLIGENCE SUMMARY
(Erase heading not required.)

Instructions regarding War Diaries and Intelligence Summaries are contained in F.S. Regs., Part II. and the Staff Manual respectively. Title Pages will be prepared in manuscript.

Place	Date 1916	Hour	Summary of Events and Information	Remarks and references to Appendices
HAUTE-AVESNES	Aug 25	6pm	Capt. W.S. FOX, RAMC, Specialist in Skin diseases XVII Corps visited his unit and discussed the treatment of 'Scabies'	WJM
	26	6pm	D.D.M.S. and D.A.D.M.S. XVII Corps inspected the Hospital	WJM
	27	6pm	Church Parade (C/E) by Rupus Hunter	WJM
	28	6pm	In accordance with Secret memo of ADMS M/S/25 Major W.C. MACAULAY R.A.M.C, T.F. has been appointed to take charge of arrangements for dealing with large numbers of Gassed Cases should they arise. A course of Instruction in "Treatment and Management of Gassed Cases" will be given by Major W.C. MACAULAY every afternoon commencing today to 21 chosen Nursing Orderlies.	WJM
	29	6pm	Lieut F. MORRES, R.A.M.C., having reported for duty is taken on the strength as from the 28th inst and is posted to "C" Section vice Lieut F.T. MORRIN transferred. (Authority D.M.S. L/E memo 28/8/16) Capt. L.W. HOWLETT RAMC has been attached for 8 days commencing today to the 2/4th Lond. Amb.	WJM

Army Form C. 2118
SHEET VI.

WAR DIARY
or
INTELLIGENCE SUMMARY
(Erase heading not required.)

Place	Date 1916	Hour	Summary of Events and Information	Remarks and references to Appendices
HAUTE-AVESNES	Aug 30	6pm	Capt. C. BURROWS has returned to this unit.	Lt/n
	31	6pm	Corpl. GREEN and 10 men have been attached to 2/6 Lond. Amb. & for July for seven days as from today and will release 11 men who will return to this unit for duty there.	

Roy
Lt. Colonel A.M.C., T.
COMMANDING 2/5th LONDON FIELD AMBULANCE.

MEDICAL.

60th Div.

Confidential

War Diary

of

2/5th London Field Ambulance.

From September 1st 1916. to September 30th. 1916

Original

Sept 1916

Vol 4

ORDERLY ROOM
No. ST 821
Date 30.9.16
2/5TH LONDON FIELD AMBULANCE
R.A.M.C.T.

COMMITTEE FOR THE
MEDICAL HISTORY OF THE WAR

Date 26 OCT. 1916

WAR DIARY

INTELLIGENCE SUMMARY

Place	Date	Hour	Summary of Events and Information	Remarks and references to Appendices
HAUTE - AVESNES	Sep 3 1916	6pm	Church Parade (C.E.) in the Dist. Theatre	25/4/17
			Staff Serg. BYLES and eleven men are detached from tomorrow for 16 days for duty with the 2/4 F. Amb. Aust⁵	25/4/17
	6th	6pm	Capt. R.E. DRAKE-BROCKMAN is detailed for duty at ANZIN with the 2/6 Aust. Amb⁵ for one week commencing today	25/4/17
			Capt. C. BURROWS is detailed as O/C Messing in addition to his other duties	25/4/17
			2067 Pte GROVER, F.C. having reported for duty from the 48th Base Depot is taken on the strength as from today and is posted to 'C' Section (AuthS. Telegram T.R. 12021 Reinforcement HAVRE 2.9.16)	25/4/17
	7	6pm	One Corporal and 10 men are attached for duty to the 2/6 Field. Amb⁵ for 7 days as from today	25/4/17
			950 Q.M. Serg. C. GILLARD and 1078 S/Serg. W. YEAXLEE went to the ranks of S/Serg. and Sergeant respectively by order of O/C R.A.M.C. Section G.H.Q. their promotions having been irregularly made, above the authorized establishment. This reversion takes as from Friday 1st Sep. 1916	25/4/17

WAR DIARY

INTELLIGENCE SUMMARY

(Erase heading not required.)

Army Form C. 2118

Instructions regarding War Diaries and Intelligence Summaries are contained in F.S. Regs., Part II. and the Staff Manual respectively. Title Pages will be prepared in manuscript.

Place	Date 1916	Hour	Summary of Events and Information	Remarks and references to Appendices
HAUTE-AVESNES	Sep 8	6pm	Pte A.E. SKUES has been sent to 2/4th Lond. Amb. vice Pte MOONEY, returns sick	15/fm
	9	6pm	2085 Pte J.H. PRIGG and 2449 Pte P.G. PADBURY have been sent today to attend Cookery Course at III'd Army Headquarters.	15/fm
			The D.D.M.S. XVII Corps and D.C. 42'nd C.C.S. visited the Hospital today	15/fm
	10	6pm	Church Parade (C.E.) in Brigd. Theatre	15/fm
			Lieut. F. MORRES having been transferred to the 56th Field Amb – a stretch of the strength as from the 8th inst. Revd G.F. SHARP C.F. is attached for rations and accommodation as from 7th inst vice Dep. G.H. FENDICK C.F. transferred to the Base.	15/fm
			T 2726 L/Cpl T.W. INGS is promoted to Unpaid Corporal dated 30 Aug. 1916	15/fm
	11	6pm	T 3266 Dvr. J. HOLMES having reported for duty is taken on the strength as from today	15/fm
	13	6pm	General BULFIN G.O.C. 60th (Lond) Div. visited the Hospital today	15/fm
	14	6pm	Capt L.W. HOWLETT in detail watched a short course of Lectures at Convalescent Camp HERMAVILLE on Sep 14th HSP at 2pm.	15/fm

Army Form C.

WAR DIARY

~~INTELLIGENCE SUMMARY~~

(Erase heading not required.)

Instructions regarding War Diaries and Intelligence Summaries are contained in F.S. Regs, Part II. and the Staff Manual respectively. Title Pages will be prepared in manuscript.

2/5th LONDON FIELD AMBULANCE T.F.

Place	Date 1916	Hour	Summary of Events and Information	Remarks and references to Appendices
HAUTE-AVESNES	Sep 14	6pm	Capt. F. ST. J. STEADMAN is detailed for duty with 24th Lond. Amb. for 8 days commencing today. One Serg. and eleven other ranks are attached as from today to the 2/4 Lond. Amb. for 8 days –	65/h/u
	15	6pm	One Serg. and 10 men are attached to the 2/6 Lond. Amb. for 7 days as from today. 2723 Serg. A.L. DOBSON and 2725 Serg. C. STIMSON 60th Bn. Tun (attached) have been granted Extra A.S.C. Corps Pay as from 1.9.16 in accordance with W.O. Letter No.9/A.S.C. 2882 (Q.M.G.5) of 1.9.16 Rev. J.H. JACKMAN C.F. (U.B) has been transferred to 4th Bde. IIIrd D.S. – Rev. A.U. MOFFAT C.F. (U.B) is attached for rations and accommodation vice Rev. J.H. JACKMAN.	65/h/u 65/h/u 65/h/u 65/h/u 65/h/u
	17	6pm	Church Parade (C.E.) in Brit. Sheets	65/h/u
	18	6pm	Capt. L.W. HOWLETT and Capt. R.E. DRAKE-BROCKMAN having been posted for duty with other units are struck off the strength as from today	65/h/u

WAR DIARY

INTELLIGENCE SUMMARY

Army Form C.2118

Place	Date 1916	Hour	Summary of Events and Information	Remarks and references to Appendices
HAUTE-AVESNES	Sep 18	6pm	Capt. W.J.T. KIMBER (2/4th Lond. Field Amb?) is temporarily attached to this Unit for duty as from today	WJSm
	20	6pm	Capt. L.L. PRESTON and Pte MOLLER recently detached for duty with the 2/2. W.C.C.S have returned to duty today	WJSm
			Capt. T.W. BOWMAN (60th Brit Suppl. Col. attached) having returned to this unit for duty is struck off the strength of this unit as from 19th inst	WJSm
	21	6pm	Major Gen. BULFIN G.O.C. 1st Staff of 60th (Lond) Div. visited the Hospital today	WJSm
			Capt. L.L. PRESTON is detailed as Officer i/c Dispensary in addition to his other duties	WJSm
	22	6pm	One N.C.O. and 10 men are attached as from Issue for 7 days for duty with 2/6 Lond Field Amb Co	WJSm
			Surgeon Genl. M. PIKE, A.M.S. JMS. 1st Army; D.D.M.S. 17th Corps and A.D.M.S 60 (Lond) Div. inspected the Hospital today	WJSm
	24	6pm	Church Parade (C.E.) in divisional Theatre	WJSm
	26	6pm	3 O.Rs. 17th Corps visited the Hospital today	WJSm
			One Sergeant and 12 O.R. attached Issue for 12 days duty with 1st 2/4 Lond. Field Amb Co	WJSm

WAR DIARY
INTELLIGENCE SUMMARY

Army Form C.2118

Place	Date	Hour	Summary of Events and Information	Remarks and references to Appendices
HAUTE-AVESNES	Sept 27 1916	6pm	1649 Pte H.H. HARDY having been evacuated from Div: area is struck off strength as from 15-9-16	15/11
	29	6pm	One Sergeant and 10 O.R. attached for duty to 2/1st Lond. Field Amb'y as from 15-9-16 for 7 days	15/11

W. Macewhacaular
Major
for Lt Colonel R.A.M.C.
COMMANDING 2/5th LONDON FIELD AMBULANCE.

140/14 F

Col. Dr

2/5 London Field Ambulance

COMMITTEE FOR THE
MEDICAL HISTORY OF THE WAR
Date 2 DEC. 1916

MEDICAL

Vol 5

2/5TH LONDON FIELD AMBULANCE.
No. ....
Date. 31/10/16

Confidential

War Diary

2/5th London Field Ambulance

From October 1st 1916. To October 31st 1916.

Original

MEDICAL
Army Form C. 2118

SHEET 1

WAR DIARY

~~INTELLIGENCE SUMMARY~~

(Erase heading not required.)

Instructions regarding War Diaries and Intelligence Summaries are contained in F. S. Regs., Part II. and the Staff Manual respectively. Title Pages will be prepared in manuscript.

2/5th LONDON FIELD AMBULANCE T.F.

Place	Date	Hour	Summary of Events and Information	Remarks and references to Appendices
HAUTE - AVESNES	1 Oct	8pm	Church Parade (C.E.) in Divl. Theatre	WJln
	2	6pm	Five men of this unit detailed for duty at Divl. Baths MAROEUIL until further notice	WJln
	3	6pm	Lieut. D.A. THOMSON R.A.M.C. having reported for duty is taken on the Strength as from today (Authy. A.D.M.S. Memo M/1658 dated 3/10/16)	WJln
			M2/174586 Corpl. A. RAMAGE 60 Divl. Supply Col. M.T. having reported for duty is taken on the Strength as from today.	WJln
	4	6pm	Lieut. A.T.P. NOWELL having reported for duty is taken on the Strength as from today (Authy. ADMS Memo M/1663 dated 4/10/16)	WJln
			1649 Pte A.H.T. HARDY having reported for duty as a Reinforcement is taken on the Strength as from 3/10/16	WJln
			Report on the result of the Examination which was held after the 3rd Cookery Course at Headquarters 3rd Army (as regards this unit):-	
			Private J. PRIGG ---- VERY GOOD COOK ---- HARD WORKER	
			" W. G. MINCHIN ---- GOOD COOK.	WJln
	6	6pm	One Sergeant and 6 men are attached as from today for duty with the 2/6 L.F.A. for seven days	WJln

WAR DIARY

INTELLIGENCE SUMMARY

Army Form C. 2118

SHEET II

Place	Date	Hour	Summary of Events and Information	Remarks and references to Appendices
HAUTE-AVESNES	Oct 7	6pm	D.D.M.S. 17th Corps visits the Hospital today. Five men details for duty at Div. Baths MAROEUIL until further notice.	W.Syn 15/tn
	8	6pm	One Sergeant and six O.R. are attached from today for 12 days for duty with the 2/4 L.F.A. Church Parade (C.E.) in Div. Theatre	W.Syn 15/tn
	11	6pm	Lieut. D.A. THOMSON and Lieut. A.J.P. NOWELL have been detailed to attend a short course on Sanitation and anti-gas measures at the Convalescent Camp HERMAVILLE at 2p.m. Oct 12 + 13 1916. Lieut. A.J.P. NOWELL having been transferred to the 8th Div. is struck off the strength as from today (auth. A.D.M.S. memo 1103 dated 10th inst) 2056 Pte A.G. DUNN having been evacuated sick from Div. Area is struck off the strength as from today (auth. A.G. letter A/6132 dated Dec 1 19/15 and Manor letter 289/94 A)	15/tn 15/tn 15/tn
	15	6pm	Church Parade (C.E.) in Div Theatre	15/tn 15/tn

Army Form C. 2118

SHEET III

WAR DIARY
~~INTELLIGENCE SUMMARY~~
(Erase heading not required.)

Instructions regarding War Diaries and Intelligence Summaries are contained in F.S. Regs, Part II. and the Staff Manual respectively. Title Pages will be prepared in manuscript.

Place	Date	Hour	Summary of Events and Information	Remarks and references to Appendices
HAUTE-AVESNES	Oct 14	6pm	2056 Pte A.G. DUNN having reported for duty as a reinforcement is taken on the strength as from this day.	AC
	19	6pm	Major W. CAMERON MACAULAY is detailed to attend at the Convalescent Camp HERMAVILLE at 2 p.m. (Eden transit ahd medical Board)	WM
	21st	6pm	Orders received that this unit is to be relieved by the 10th Canadian Fd Amb't the 60th Div is being about to be relieved by the 3rd Canadian Div. Major W.C. MACAULAY is granted special leave Oct 22nd – Nov 1st & has left this evening for BOULOGNE. Capt SWADGE of 10th Canadian Fd Amb has reported to this unit in advance of 10th Can. Fd Amb.	Fd Amb't See RAMC Op Orders no 3. RC AC
	23rd	6pm	Major PHILP O/c 10th Can. Fd Amb; with 2 sections of his personnel, has assumed this morning, & takes over from this unit this evening. 4 wagons (ambulance, 3 horse (install with wagons) orderlies were left in our charge with orders to accompany 2. 150th Bde. (to accompany Batth in line) & moved by this unit is ordered to vacate this area 2 morrow morning.	RC See RAMC Op Orders no 3. RC

Wt. W393/826 1,000,000 4/15 J.B.C. & A. A.D.S.S./Forms/C.2118.

Army Form C. 2118

SHEET IV

WAR DIARY or INTELLIGENCE SUMMARY

(Erase heading not required.)

Instructions regarding War Diaries and Intelligence Summaries are contained in F.S. Regs., Part II. and the Staff Manual respectively. Title Pages will be prepared in manuscript.

[Stamp: 5TH LONDON FIELD AMBULANCE T.F.]

Place	Date	Hour	Summary of Events and Information	Remarks and references to Appendices
PENIN.	Oct. 24th	6 p.m.	This unit moved to-day under Brigade (180th) orders * to PENIN, where a Reception Hospital has been established for the Brigade — A rear party (one Capt. & 3 men) were left at HAUTE MESNES in charge of baggage belonging to 24th, 25th & 26th Field Ambulances by instructions of A.D.M.S. — Being attached to 10th Canadian Field Amb. for rations &c —	* 180 L/F Bde. order No 18. R.C.
	25th	6 p.m.	Sick in Hospital evacuated to St POL. Equipment overhauled —	R.C.
MONCHEAUX	26th	6 p.m.	The unit moved on to MONCHEAUX under orders * from the order already issued /No 18 * by 180th Bde. A reception hospital for the Bde. has been established at this place —	* R.C.
	27th	6 p.m.	Sick in Hospital evacuated to St POL & TREVENT. Orders received from A.D.M.S. to despatch all mechanical transport to Pte 56 "Div" at LESTREM to-morrow morning. Orders from 180th Bde. to move to REMAISNIL to-morrow. The ambulance wagons detailed to accompany battalions have now returned to this unit.	R.C.
REMAISNIL.	28th	6 a.m.	All mechanical transport went off in accordance with orders to 56th Div. at LESTREM * This unit moved to REMAISNIL to-day, in accordance with 180th L/F. Bde. Order No 19.*	* See attached R.C.

1875 Wt. W593/826 1,000,000 4/15 J.B.C. & A. A.D.S.S./Forms/C. 2118.

WAR DIARY

Army Form C. 2118

SHEET 1

Place	Date	Hour	Summary of Events and Information	Remarks and references to Appendices
LE MEILLARD	Oct 29th	6p.m.	The unit moved to-day under Brigade Orders + to LE MEILLARD. I have now only 2 ambulance wagons at my disposal, both horse-drawn, my 3rd wagon having been smashed up in an accident this morning (horses bolted). There are 34 men in the Reception Hosp: formed at this place, picked up on the line of march (chiefly suffering from exhaustion, + under rest) – Not more than 2 men of this unit have fallen out during the recent moves.	+180 "E.P. Bde." as Bl. No 20 R.C.
	30th	6p.m.	The Hospital has been evacuated to-day, about 7/8ths to meet Convoy, all 7/8 J & remainder (except 3 men still retained) to Casualty Clearing Station at DOULLENS.	R.C. R.C.
	31st	6p.m.	The unit had a route march this morning.	

Rosser
O/C 2/5 Lond Fd Amb.

Appendix.

War Diary

2/5th London Field Ambulance

October 1st — October 31st 1916

SECRET.   COPY NO. 8

180th INFANTRY BRIGADE ORDER NO. 18.

1. The 180th Infantry Brigade will march to the HOUVIN - HOUVIGNEUL area in accordance with attached March Table.

2. The 180th Machine Gun Company and the Personnel of the 180th Trench Mortar Battery will march with the 2/17th Bn. London Regt. and will ascertain starting point from the latter Battalion. Arrangements are being made for the transport of the guns of the 180th Trench Mortar Battery by Motor Lorry.

3. Battalion Transport will accompany Battalions.

4. The 1/6th Field Company, R.E., and the 2/5th Field Ambulance will come under the orders of the 180th Infantry Brigade for billeting and march routes from 24th and 25th inst. respectively.

5. Billeting parties (1 Officer and 4 O.R., per Battalion, and 1 Officer and 2 O.R. for other Units) will proceed in advance on same day as Unit moves and arrange billets in areas allotted, details of which are being sent to Units. Army Form W.3401 and Army Book 397 must be completed and handed to the Mayor before Units march out from their billets.

6. One Motor or horse Ambulance from 2/5th Field Ambulance will be attached to each Battalion until the new area is reached when further orders for their disposal will be issued.

7. Refilling points as laid down in S.O/129/13 forwarded under Brigade No. A.943/5 dated 22nd October 1916.

8. Time of arrival in new billets after each move will be reported to Brigade Headquarters by cyclist orderly or telegraph if available.

9. Brigade Headquarters closes at MONT ST. ELOY at 11 a.m. 25th October 1916 and opens at HOUVIN HOUVIGNEUL the same hour.

10. ACKNOWLEDGE.

ADV. BDE. H.Q.
23rd October 1916.

Captain,
BRIGADE MAJOR,
180th Infantry Brigade.

Issued to at 1 p.m. :-

    Copy No. 1. 2/17th Bn. London Regt.
           2. 2/18th   -do-
           3. 2/19th   -do-
           4. 2/20th   -do-
           5. 180th Machine Gun Company.
           6. 180th Trench Mortar Battery.
           7. 1/6th Field Company, R.E.
           8. 2/5th Field Ambulance.
           9. No. 3 Signal Section, R.E.
          10. No. 3 Company, A.S.C.
          11.   -do-
          12. 60th (London) Division.
          13. 179th Infantry Brigade.
          14. Rear Brigade H.Q.
          15.   -do-
          16. War Diary.
          17.   -do-
          18. File.

MARCH TABLE.

DATE.	UNIT.	FROM.	TO.	TIME OF START.	ROUTE.	REMARKS.
23rd Oct.	2/20th Bn. London Rgt.	BOIS DES ALLEUX.	PENIN.	9 a.m.		
	2/20th Bn. London Rgt.	PENIN.	HOUVIN-HOUVIGNEUL.	9 a.m.		
24th Oct.	2/5th Field Ambulance.	HAUTE-AVESNES.	PENIN.	9 a.m.	ACQ - Road Junction ACQ-ST.POL Road in HAUTE-AVESNES - SAVY - BERLES - PENIN - MAIZIERES.	
25th Oct.	2/19th Bn. London Rgt.	BOIS DES ALLEUX.	PENIN.	9 a.m.		
	BRIGADE H.Q.	MT. ST. ELOY.	HOUVIN-HOUVIGNEUL.	8 a.m.		
26th Oct.	H.Q. & 2 Coys. 2/19th.	PENIN.	CANETTEMONT.	9 a.m.		
	2 Coys. 2/19th Bn.	PENIN.	HOUVIN-HOUVIGNEUL.	9 a.m.		
	1/6th Field Coy. R.E.	PENIN.	MONCHEAUX.	9 a.m.		
	2/5th Field Ambulance.	PENIN.	MONCHEAUX.	10 a.m.		
	2/17th Bn. London Rgt.	ECOIVRES.	PENIN.	9 a.m.		To march with 2/17th.
	180th Machine Gun Coy.	ECOIVRES.	PENIN.	9 a.m.		
	180th Trench Mortar By.	MT. ST. ELOY.	PENIN.	9 a.m.		
	2/18th Bn. London Regt.	ACQ.	MAGNICOURT.	8 a.m.		By bus.
27th Oct.	2/17th Bn. London Rgt.	PENIN.	REBREUVIETTE.	9 a.m.		
	180th Trench Mortar By.	PENIN.	HOUVIN-HOUVIGNEUL.	9 a.m.		
	180th Machine Gun Coy.	PENIN.	HOUVIN-HOUVIGN UL.	9 a.m.		

MARCH TABLE.

DATE.	UNIT.	FROM.	TO.	TIME OF START.	ROUTE.	REMARKS.
23rd Oct.	2/20th Lond. Regt.	BOIS DES ALLEUX	PENIN	9 a.m.		
24th Oct.	2/20th Lond. Regt.	PENIN	HOUVIN-HOUVIGNEUL	9 a.m.		
	2/5th Field Amb.	HOUT-AVESNES	PENIN	9 a.m.		
25th Oct.	2/19th Lond. Regt.	BOIS DES ALLEUX	PENIN	9 a.m.		
	BRIG. D. H.Q.	PETIT ST ELOY	PETIT ST ELOY			
26th Oct.	BRIG. D. H.Q.	PETIT ST ELOY	REBREUVE	8 a.m.	AQQ - Road junction ARRAS ST POL. Road in HAUTE-AVESNES - SAVY - BERLES - PENIN - MAIZIERES.	
	H.Q. and 2 Coys 2/19th Lond.	PENIN	CANETTEMONT	9 a.m.		
	1 Coy 2/19th.	PENIN	HOUVIN-HOUVIGNEUL	9 a.m.		
	1 Coy 2/19th.	PENIN	REBREUVE	9 a.m.		
	1/6th Field Coy R.E.	PENIN	CANETTEMONT	9 a.m.		
	2/5th Field Amb.	PENIN	CANETTEMONT	10 a.m.		
	2/17th Lond. Regt.	COIVRES	PENIN	9 a.m.		
	180th Machine G.C.	COIVRES	PENIN	9 a.m.		
	180th Trench .By	O. T ST LOY	PETIT BOURET	9 a.m.		
	H.Q. & 3 Coys 2/18th	GQ	PETIT BOURET	8 a.m.		
	1 Coy 2/18th Lond.	GQ	REBREUVE	8 a.m.		
27 Oct.	2/17th Lond. Regt	PENIN	MAGNICOURT	9 a.m.		) To march with
	180th Trench .By	PENIN	MAGNICOURT	9 a.m.		) 2/17th.
	180th Machine G.C.	PENIN	REBREUVE	9 a.m.		) By Bus
						) do.

O.C. 1/5th Field Co. R.E.
2/5th London Field Ambulance.

Reference this Office letter of this morning enclosing amended march table, you will be moving to-morrow to MONCHEAUX and not CANETTEMONT as stated therein.

H.W.Chives

Captain.
for STAFF CAPTAIN.
180th Infantry Brigade.

REAR BDE. H.Q.
25th Oct. 1916.

SECRET.

Copy. No. 8

180th Infantry Brigade Order No. 19.

(Ref. Map LENS 1/100,000)

1. The 180th Infantry Brigade will move into the new area on 28th October 1916 in accordance with attached March Table.

2. The Brigade Starting Point will be CROSS ROADS at T in GRAND BOURET.

3. Units will march in the following order -

   (1) 2/17th London Regt. and 180th T.M.Battery.
   (2) 2/20th London Regt.
   (3) 2/19th London Regt.
   (4) 180th M.G.Coy.
   (5) 2/18th London Regt.
   (6) 180th Infantry Brigade H.Q.
   (7) 1/6th Field Coy.
   (8) 2/5th Field Ambulance.
   (9) No.3 Coy. A.S.C.

4. Battalions will march followed by 1st Line Transport and baggage wagons.

5. Battalions will halt for 10 minutes previous to each clock hour, no matter at what time they start.

6. One Motor or horse Ambulance will be detailed by 2/5th Field Ambulance to accompany each Battalion until the new area is reached.

7. Billeting parties will proceed in advance on same day as unit moves and arrange billets in areas allotted, details of which are being issued separately.

8. Refilling points on DOULLENS - AUXI LE CHATEAU Road between FROHEN LE GRAND and road junction about 2 miles W. of that place.

9. Attention is directed to Divisional Standing Order, Page 10.

10. Brigade Headquarters close at REBREUVE at 10.a.m. 28th October 1916, after which hour reports will be sent to the head of the column.
    On conclusion of march Brigade Headquarters will be established at REMAISNIL Chateau.

11. ACKNOWLEDGE.

Captain.
BRIGADE MAJOR.
180th Infantry Brigade.

BRIGADE H.Q.
27th October 1916.

Over -

Issued to :-

Copy No. 1. 2/17th Bn. London Regt.
2. 2/18th -do-
3. 2/19th -do-
4. 2/20th -do-
5. 180th Machine Gun Company.
6. 180th Trench Mortar Battery.
7. 1/6th Field Company, R.E.
8. 2/5th Field Ambulance.
9. No. 3 Signal Section, R.E.
10. No. 3 Company A.S.C.
11. -do-
12. 60th Division "A"
13. 60th Division "G"
14. C.R.E. 60th Division.
15. A.D.M.S. 60th Division.
16. War Diary.
17. -do-
18. File.

MARCH TABLE.

UNIT.	FROM.	TO.	TIME OF STARTING.	STARTING POINT.	ROUTE.	REMARKS.
Brigade H.Q.	REBREUVE.	REMAISNIL.	10.5 a.m.	Road junction of FREVENT - REBREUVIETTE and REBREUVE - BOUQUEMAISON roads.	HOUVIN HOUVIGNEUL, Road junction S.E. of CANETTEMONT - GRAND BOURET.	
2/17th Bn. London Regt.	MAGNICOURT.	BONNIERES	7.40 a.m.	Road junction N.W. end of MAGNICOURT.		
180th T.M.B.	-do-	-do-	-do-	-do-		March with 2/17
2/18th Bn. London Regt.	PT. FOURET REBREUVE	OUTREBOIS	10.10 a.m.	Cross roads by T in GRAND BOURET.		
180th M.G.C.	REBREUVE.	OUTREBOIS.	10 a.m.	Road junction REBREUVE - BOUQUEMAISON & FREVENT - REBREUVIETTE Roads.		
2/19th Bn. London Regt.	CANETTEMONT HOUVIN HOUVIGNEUL REBREUVE.	MEZEROLLES.	9.6.a.m.	Road junction S.E. end of CANETTEMONT.		
2/20th Bn. London Regt.	HOUVIN HOUVIGNEUL.	BONNIERES.	8.25 a.m.	Road junction ½ mile N. of V in HOUVIN.		
1/6th Field Coy. R.E.	MONCHEAUX.	BONNIERES	8.30 a.m.	Road junction ½ mile S.E. of E in MONCHEAUX.		
2/5th Field Amb.	MONCHEAUX.	REMAISNIL.	8.35 a.m.	-do-		
No. 3 Coy. A.S.C.	MONCHEAUX.	OUTREBOIS.	8.40 a.m.	-do-		

N.B. Troops will not be brought back to the Unit Starting Point, but will join their units on route.

SECRET.   Copy No. 8

180th Infantry Brigade Order No. 20.

(Ref. Map LENS 1/100,000).

1. The 180th Infantry Brigade will move into the BERNAVILLE area on 29th October 1916 in accordance with attached March Table.

2. The Brigade Starting Point will be Road junction at North End of LE MEILLARD.

3. Units will march in the following order. -

    (1). 2/19th Bn. London Regt.
    (2). 2/18th   -do-
    (3). 180th Machine Gun Company.
    (4). 2/17th Bn. London Regt. and 180th T.M. Battery.
    (5). 2/20th   -do-
    (6). 180th Infantry Brigade H.Q.
    (7). 1/6th Field Coy. R.E.
    (8). 2/5th Field Ambulance.
    (9). No. 3 Coy. A.S.C.

4. Battalions will march followed by 1st Line Transport and baggage wagons.

5. Battalions will halt for 10 minutes previous to each clock hour, no matter at what time they start.

6. Billeting Parties for BERNAVILLE and VACQUERIE will report to Town Major at his office opposite the Hotel de Ville.
    Billeting Parties for BERNEUIL will report to the Officer of the Commandant, Reserve Army School. Billeting parties of other Units will proceed in advance on same day as Unit moves and arrange billets in area allotted, details of which are being issued separately.

7. 2/5th Field Ambulance will march as a Unit to LE MEILLARD after which they will detach 2 Ambulance Wagons to follow the remainder of the column until Units reach their destination.

8. Refilling point on the road between BERNAVILLE and FIENVILLERS.

9. Attention is directed to Divisional Standing Order, Page 10.

10. Brigade Headquarters close at REMAISNIL at 9 a.m. 29th October 1916, after which hour reports will be sent to the head of the column.
    On conclusion of march Brigade Headquarters will be established at LE MEILLARD.

11. ACKNOWLEDGE.

                                              Captain,
                                            Brigade Major,
                                         180th Infantry Brigade.

BRIGADE H.Q.
28th October 1916.

Issued to :-

Copy No. 1. 2/17th Bn. London Regt.
2. 2/18th -do-
3. 2/19th -do-
4. 2/20th -do-
5. 180th Machine Gun Company.
6. 180th Trench Mortar Battery.
7. 1/6th Field Company, R.E.
8. 2/5th Field Ambulance.
9. No. 3 Signal Section, R.E.
10. No. 3 Company, A.S.C.
11. -do-
12. 60th Division "A"
13. 60th Division "G"
14. C.R.E. 60th Division.
15. A.D.M.S. 60th Division.
16. War Diary.
17. -do-
18. File.

MARCH TABLE.

Unit.	FROM	TO.	TIME OF STARTING.	STARTING POINT.	ROUTE.	REMARKS.
Brigade H.Q.	REMAISNIL.	LE MEILLARD.	9.22.a.m.	Road junction REMAISNIL - BARLY & REMAISNIL - MEZEROLLES Roads.		
2/17th London Regt.	BONNIERES	BERNAVILLE	7.38.a.m.	BONNIERES - BARLY & REBREUVIETTE - VILLERS L'HOPITAL Roads.		
180th T.M.Battery.	do.	do.	do.	do.		March with 2/17th.
2/18th London Regt.	OUTREBOIS	H.Q. & 3 Coys VACQUERIE. 1 Coy. GORGES.	8.47.a.m.	Road junction S. of S in GOURCELLES.		
180th M.G.Coy.	do.	BERNEUIL.	9.5.a.m.	do.		
2/19th London Regt.	MEZEROLLES.	BERNEUIL.	9.20.a.m.	Road junction LE MEILLARD - MEZEROLLES & OUTREBOIS - FROHEN LE PETIT Roads.		
2/20th London Regt.	BONNIERES.	HEUZECOURT.	7.45.a.m.	Road junction BONNIERES - BARLY & REBREUVIETTE - VILLERS L'HOPITAL Roads.		
1/6th Field Co.R.E.	BONNIERES.	LE MEILLARD.	8.4.a.m.	do.		
2/5th Field Amb.	REMAISNIL.	do.	9.30.a.m.	Road junction REMAISNIL - BARLY - REMAISNIL - MEZEROLLES Roads.		
No.3 Coy. A.S.C.	OUTREBOIS	BERNAVILLE	9.35.a.m.	Road junction S. of S in COURCELLES.		

REMAISNIL - MEZEROLLES - LE MEILLARD - BERNAVILLE.

Units will leave this route at the nearest point to their respective Billeting Areas.

SECRET. *for War Diary.* COPY No. 2.

R.A.M.C. OPERATION ORDER No 3.

October 20th 1916.

1. The 60th Division (less Artillery) will be relieved by the 3rd Canadian Division (less Artillery) during the period 23 - 26 October, 1916.

   The 60th Division is to be concentrated in the new area by midnight 27 - 28 October 1916.

2. Os./C. Field Ambulances will hand over the Command of the Medical Arrangements of their respective areas on completion of relief. Completion of relief of each Unit to be reported to this Office.

3. March Table and Schedule of reliefs will be issued later.

4. Refilling Points will be detailed later.

5. The Command of the Front remains in the hands of the G.O.C. 60th Division until 10 am 26th inst., at which hour 60th Divl. H.Q. will open at LE CAUROY.

6. Receipts will be received for any stores, including Red Cross Stores, from Os./C. incoming Field Ambulances in accordance with H.Q. memorandum C/371 of the 19th inst., copy being forwarded to this Office.

7. Patients left in 60th Divisional Field Ambulances will be shown in the A. & D. Books as "Transferred to Canadian Field Ambulances," and Nominal Roll with all necessary particulars will be handed to the Os./C. respective relieving Field Ambulances.

8. Details to be arranged by Os./C. concerned.

9. Acknowledge.

E.B. Dowsett
COLONEL
A.D.M.S. 60th (LONDON) DIVISION.

Copy No 1. O.C. 2/4th Lon. Fd. Amb.
"   2. O.C. 2/5th Lon. Fd. Amb.
"   3. O.C. 2/6th Lon. Fd. Amb.
"   4. War Diary.
"   5. Duplicate War Diary.
"   6. File.

For War Diary

SECRET.

Copy No. 2.

60th DIVISION R.A.M.C. OPERATION ORDER No. 4

October 22nd 1916.

Ref. Map LENS - Sheet 11.

1. The reliefs of Field Ambulances and their marches to new Area will be carried out in accordance with Tables "A" & "B" attached.
   All arrangements as to guides to front area will be made by Os.C. Field Ambulances concerned.

2. All incoming parties of Canadian Field Ambulance on 23rd inst. will be rationed and billeted by the respective London Field Ambulance to which they are attached, till relief is complete.
   Arrangements will be made for the billeting by closing up the patients into fewer huts for night of 23rd - 24th October, 1916, and utilising a hut for the personnel.

3. The actual destination and billeting accommodation of each Field Ambulance in its new area must be forthwith ascertained by Os.C. from the respective brigades to which they are attached (vide Table "B").

4. A temporary receiving station for sick will be opened by each Field Ambulance immediately on arrival in the new area, and the Brigade Offices in the respective areas informed.
   All sick not likely to be well in 24 hours will be transferred direct to No. 12 Stationary Hospital, ST. POL.

5. Separate instructions are being issued re Field Ambulance Stores. See Operation Order No. 3 re receipts.

6. On evening of 22nd inst. each Field Ambulance will send four Ambulance Wagons, with orderlies, (3 horsed & 1 motor) - one to each of the Wagons lines of the Battalions of the respective Brigades to which the Field Ambulances are attached. These will remain with the Battalions till arrival in New Area, when they will return to their Units.
   The wagons will be under the orders of the M.O's of Units, and are for the purpose of collecting sick on line of route. Before leaving, Os.C. Field Ambulances will instruct the wagon orderlies that they are only to pick up men possessing a chit signed by the M.O. of the Unit.

7. Command of the Medical Arrangements of present 60th Division Area will be handed over to A.D.M.S. 3rd Canadian Division at Noon 24th inst.

8. Acknowledge.

Colonel.
A.D.M.S. 60th (London) Division.

```
Copy No. 1    2/4th Lon. Fd. Amb.
Copy No. 2    2/5th Lon. Fd. Amb.
Copy No. 3    2/6th Lon. Fd. Amb.
Copy No. 4    War Diary.
Copy No. 5    Duplicate War Diary.
Copy No. 6    File.
Copy No. 7    Headquarters.
```

TABLE A

RELIEF TABLE OF FIELD AMBULANCES OF 60th (LONDON) DIVISION.

Unit	Proceeding to	Time of arrival	Relieves	Proceeding to	Time of Departure
8th CANADIAN FIELD AMBULANCE. 1 Officer) 4 N.C.O's) 40 men)	ANZIN and Right Sector Trenches via HAUTE AVESNES.	about noon at HAUTE AVESNES Oct.23rd 1918	2/6th Lon Fd Amb personnel at Adv. Dressing Station and in front of same.	HAUTE AVESNES	When relieved
9th CANADIAN FIELD AMBULANCE. 1 Officer) 4 N.C.O's) 40 men)	AUX RIETZ and left and centre Sectors trenches via ECOIVRES.	about noon at ECOIVRES Oct.23rd 1918	2/4th Lon Fd amb. personnel at Adv. Dressing Station and infront of same.	ECOIVRES.	When relieved
8th CANADIAN FIELD AMBULANCE. 2 Sections.	HAUTE AVESNES	evening of Oct.23rd 1918	Whole of 2/6th Lon Fd. Ambulance.	New Area	Morning of Oct.24th 1918
9th CANADIAN FIELD AMBULANCE 2 Sections	ECOIVRES	evening of Oct.23rd 1918	Whole of 2/4th Lon Fd. Ambulance	New Area	Morning of Oct.24th 1918
10th CANADIAN FIELD AMBULANCE 2 Sections.	HAUTE AVESNES	evening of Oct.23rd 1918	Whole of 2/5th Lon Fd. Ambulance.	New Area	Morning of Oct.24th 1918

H.Q. 60th Division.
October 22nd 1918

A.D.M.S. 60th (London) Division.
Colonel

TABLE "D".

LE CAUROY	... ...	Div. H.Q.

179 Bde. Area.		Troops.
SIBIVILLE	... Bde. H.Q. ⎫	
BUNEVILLE	⎬	179 Inf. Bde.
MONTS EN TERNOIS	⎬	2/4 Fd. Co. R.E.
MONCHAUX	⎬	2/4 Fd. Amb.
SERICOURT	⎬	Det. Train.
HONVAL	⎭	

REBREUVE is added to this area for the night of the 28/29th.

180 Bde. Area.		Troops.
ROUVIN	... Bde. H.Q. ⎫	180 Inf. Bde.
HOUVIGNEUL	⎬	1/6 Fd. Co. R.E.
SAINT IMONT	⎬	2/5 Fd. Amb.
MAGNICOURT	⎭	Det. Train.

REBREUVIETTE, ROZIERE and BROUILLY are added to this area for the night of the 28/29th.

181 Bde. Area.		Troops.
BERLENCOURT	... Bde. H.Q. ⎫	181 Inf. Bde.
LAIZIERES	⎬	3/3 Fd. Co. R.E.
SARS LES BOIS	⎬	2/6 Fd. Amb.
DENIER	⎬	Det. Train.
GOUY EN TERNOIS	⎭	

BERLE-WANIN is added to this area for the night of the 28/29th.

LIENCOURT	... ...	1/12 L.N.Lancs. R.
GRAND BOURET	... ...	60 Div. Supply Column. 60 Mob. Vet. Sec.
WANIN	... ...	60 Div. Train.
LE CAUROY	... ...	60 San: Sec.

MEDICAL

— Confidential —

War Diary

of

3/5 London Field Ambulance. R.A.M.C. — 60th London Division.

From November 1st 1916 To November 30th 1916

COMMITTEE FOR THE
MEDICAL HISTORY OF THE WAR
Date 30 APR. 1917

WAR DIARY or INTELLIGENCE SUMMARY

Army Form C. 2118.

Place	Date 1916	Hour	Summary of Events and Information	Remarks and references to Appendices
LE MEILLARD	Nov 1	6pm	Notifies that all A.S.C. personnel have been posted from T.F. to Regular Army. New Regimental numbers allotted accordingly. — Auth'y. A.C.I. N°1699 and A.S.C. Records. Woolwich Dockyard C.R./29542/V/96 dated 16 Oct 1916	~~Appendix~~ IV 1/pm
	2	6pm	The Field Ambulance was inspected by A.D.M.S. 60 D.S'' today	15/pm
			Major W. CAMERON MACAULAY returned to duty today from special leave to England	15/pm
BUSSUS-BUSSUEL	3	6pm	Unit moved with 780 Inf. Bde. from LE MEILLARD to BUSSUS-BUSSUEL by route march today. 1 Amb. wagon detailed to follow 2/20 Bn L.R. and 1 to follow 2/18th Bn L.R. The 2 motor ambulances of N°26 M.A.C. which were attached to this unit on 31st ult. returned to their unit under instructions of A.D.M.S.	15/pm
			7 Motor amb. wagons and 2 motor cycles together with 13 N.C.O. and men of N°56 S.C. joined for duty today	15/pm
			Reception Hospital established at BUSSUS-BUSSUEL today	15/pm
			Church Parade C.E. held in the Chateau.	15/pm
	5	6pm	2067 Pte GROVER, F.C. having been evacuated sick out to the But area is taken off the strength of this unit as from yesterday	15/pm
			Instructions received today that 60 D.S. will be reorganised under War Establishment Part XII "SALONIKA 4" for Service overseas.	15/pm

Army Form C. 2118.

2/5TH LONDON FIELD AMBULANCE.

WAR DIARY or INTELLIGENCE SUMMARY.
(Erase heading not required.)

Instructions regarding War Diaries and Intelligence Summaries are contained in F.S. Regs., Part II. and the Staff Manual respectively. Title pages will be prepared in manuscript.

Place	Date 1916	Hour	Summary of Events and Information	Remarks and references to Appendices
BUSSUS-BUSSUEL	Nov 6	8pm	4 Limbered G.S. Wagons returned to No 3 Coy A.S.C. complete with horses, harness, fittings &c and also 4 drivers who are struck off the strength as from today viz :- T4/239324 Dr. PUNTT, J T4/239311 Dr. GILL, F.G. T4/239309 " DOWLING, R.S. T4/239342 " GRANT, A.H.	WJW
	7	8pm	5 men detailed for duty at Baths established in the village under supervision of O.C. Divl Baths	WJW
	8	8pm	The undermentioned Officers, N.C.O. and men have been granted leave to England from 8.11.16 to 12.11.16 Lieut. Col. R CORFE, Capt. F. ST J. STEADMAN, Serg. Major A.F. BAUM, Serg. A. ALLGROVE, Ptes DAWSON, LLOYD, WILSON Lieut. W.A. HOTSON is detailed as M.O. to 2/19 Bn. L.R. until 13th inst. when R.M.O. returns from leave All equipment attached. Indents submitted for all increments and deficient articles	WJW WJW WJW
	10	8pm	Major W. CAMERON MACAULAY, Lieut. L. LESLIE and Serg. YEAXLEE attended a lecture and demonstration on the Small Box Respirator at GORENFLOS at 10 a.m. Today M.O., N.C.O., men & O.C. attended a lecture at Headqrs 247 B^s L.R. at 11.15 a.m. today on "The Method of Scoring Post Animals."	WJW WJW

2353 Wt. W2544/4454 700,000 5/15 D. D. & L. A.D.S.S./Forms/C. 2118.

WAR DIARY or INTELLIGENCE SUMMARY

Army Form C. 2118.

25TH LONDON FIELD AMBULANCE

Place	Date 1916	Hour	Summary of Events and Information	Remarks and references to Appendices
BUSSUS - BUSSUEL	10 Nov.	6pm	2149 Pte PADBURY, P.G. evacuated sick out of D.I. area and struck off Strength. Capt. C. BURROWS is detailed as M.O. to 2/17 Bn and 2/20 Bn L.R. during the absence on leave until 14th inst of the respective R.M.O. Capt. L.L. PRESTON having been transferred to 2nd C.C.S. is struck off the Strength of this unit dates Nov. 9. 1916 (Auth. A.D.M.S. wire M/1176 9.11.16) 1148 L/Cpl. MOORE, A.H. having been evacuated sick from the D.I. area is struck off the strength of this unit (Exeter)	WJM WJM WJM WJM
	11	8pm	The following officers have reported for temporary duty with this unit Captain D.F.A. NEILSON, Capt. C.H. NEWTON, Lieut. R.H.S. MARSHALL and are taken on the strength for rations and billets (Auth. A.D.M.S. memo hereunder) Lieut R.H.S. MARSHALL takes over medical charge of 2/17th and 2/20 Bn L.R. vice Capt. C. BURROWS who returns to his unit Lieut. D.A. THOMSON having been transferred to 4th D.S. is struck of the strength as from today (auth. A.D.M.S. Telegram M 1346)	WJM WJM WJM
	12	6pm	Capt. C.H. NEWTON who was temporarily attached to this unit for duty is W.A.S. transferred for permanent duty with the 246th Lond. Amb= as from today	WJM

WAR DIARY or INTELLIGENCE SUMMARY

Army Form C. 2118.

25TH LONDON FIELD AMBULANCE.

Place	Date	Hour	Summary of Events and Information	Remarks and references to Appendices
BUSSUS-BUSSUEL	19/6 hr			
	12	6pm	Capt. D.F.S. NEILSON who was temporarily attached to this unit for duty is now transferred for permanent duty as M.O. 2/13th Bn L.R. as from today. Capt. & Q.M. A.J. NAYLOR having been evacuated sick by order of the A.D.M.S. 60 Divn is struck off the strength of this unit as from today (Auth. A.D.M.S. telegram memo M 1364 of 11/11/16 & Helgrs XV Corps). Capt. D.N. HARDCASTLE having reported for duty is taken on the strength of this unit (Auth. ADMS memo) 23 Riding Horses and 44 draught mules taken today into mallein test.	15/hr
	13	6pm		15/hr
	14	6pm	Lieut R GOVAN having reported for duty is taken on the strength of this unit as from today. 2149 Pte PADBURY P.G. having reported as a reinforcement is taken on the strength as from today — Rev. G.F. SHARP, C.F., attached to this unit for rations and accommodation having been transferred to the base is struck off the strength as from the 13th inst.	15/hr 15/hr
	15	6pm	The following N.C.O. and men having reported for duty as a reinforcement	15/hr

WAR DIARY
INTELLIGENCE SUMMARY

Army Form C. 2118.

2/5TH LONDON FIELD AMBULANCE

Place	Date 1916	Hour	Summary of Events and Information	Remarks and references to Appendices
BUSSUS BUSSUEL	NOV 15	cont.d 6pm	are taken on the strength as from today:— 2847 Cpl NASHWALDER, 2238 Pte HAWKINS, 1948 Pte BROOK, 790 Pte HUSBAND, W.H. 1817 Pte MOORE, E.R., 1869 Pte TRUEMAN, E.W., 1658 Pte TERRY, F.G. 543 Pte HART, E.A., 500 Pte WELLS, W.H., 759 Pte JONES, W.H., 294 Pte KILSON, R.H., 76648 Pte ALLEN, W.	WJm WJm WJm WJm
	16	6pm	Lieut. & Q.M. N.E. HILL having reported for duty is taken on the strength as from today. 294 Pte (Acting Lance-Corpl.) KILTON, R.H. is promoted to rank of Lance Corporal.	
	17	6pm	Capt. & Lt. NEWTON having reported for duty is taken on the strength as from today. Capt. C. BURROWS having been evacuated sick to the Base is struck off the strength as from this date. 279 Q.M. Sergt VILE, A. having resumed duty at the A.D.M.S.'s Office is struck off the strength as from today. 1636 Sergt WILLCOCKS having reported from the A.D.M.S. Office	

WAR DIARY

Army Form C. 2118.

2/5TH LONDON FIELD AMBULANCE.

Place	Date 1916	Hour	Summary of Events and Information	Remarks and references to Appendices
BUSSUS BUSSUEL	Nov 17	cont. 6 p.m.	To be taken on the strength as from today. — The following men having returned for duty, are taken on the strength as from today: — 2114 Pte BAKER, A.F., 2112 Pte EVERARD, E.E., 2290 Pte GARROD, R.S., 2233 Pte READ, C.E. The following promotions take effect as from today: — 950 S/Sergt. E. GILLARD to be Quarter Master Sergeant. 1078 Sergt. W.J. YEAXLEE to be Staff-Sergeant. 2307 Pte SMITH, F.W. has been awarded 28 days F.P. No 2 for "Neglect to obey an order".	WDfm WDfm WDfm WDfm
	18	6 p.m.	Major W. CAMERON MACAULAY, Lieut R. GOVAN (N.P.2) Lieut L. LESLIE and 122 O.R. left by route march for LONGPRÉ at 8.30 a.m. entrained at 9 p.m. and left for MARSEILLES at 11 p.m. nearly 9 hours after Scheduletime. Lieut-Col. R. CORFE, Capt F. ST. J. STEADMAN, Capt D.V. HARDCASTLE, Capt A.H. NEWTON, Lieut W.A. HOTSON, Lieut R.H.S. MARSHALL Lieut W.E. HILL (P.M.) 65 O.R. 67 animals and 3 vehicles left by route march at 7 p.m. (amended time) for LONGPRÉ entrained and left for MARSEILLES at 9.55 a.m. 19th inst. (16 hours after Scheduled time.) See * below	Appendix I WDfm Afix I WDfm

WAR DIARY
or
~~INTELLIGENCE SUMMARY~~

(Erase heading not required.)

Army Form C. 2118.

Instructions regarding War Diaries and Intelligence Summaries are contained in F.S. Regs. Part II. and the Staff Manual respectively. Title pages will be prepared in manuscript.

Place	Date 1916	Hour	Summary of Events and Information	Remarks and references to Appendices
BUSSUS BUSSUEL	Nov. 18	6 p.m.	At LONGPRÉ Lieut H.M. LAMBERT and 175 O.R. A.S.C. having reported for duty with the unit are taken on the Strength.	WJ/m
		*	Owing to lack of accommodation in the train originally prepared for this unit Capt. F. ST J. STEADMAN, Lieut. R.H.S. MARSHALL and 185 O.R. were detained by the R.T.O LONGPRÉ. These were eventually got away in 3 separate parties without an Officer in charge.	App x I
	19-20		Spent in train	WJ/m WJ/m
MARSEILLES	21	6am	Major W. CAMERON MACAULAY, Lieut R. GOVAN (N°2) Lieut. L. LESLIE detrained at MARSEILLES at 7.1 a.m. and proceeded by route march to Camp (CARCASONNE) LIEUT-COL R.CORFE, Capt. D.N. HARDCASTLE, Capt A.H. NEWTON, Lieut. W.A. HOTSON, Lieut t.Q.M W.E. HILL 5 Lieut. H.M. LAMBERT (A.S.C.) and 107 O.R. 67 animals and 3 vehicles detrained at MARSEILLES at 12.50 (noon) and proceeded by route march to LA VALENTINE Camp	WJ/m WJ/m
	12	midnight	80 N.C.O. and men A.S.C. detrained and proceeded by route march to LA VALENTINE Camp.	WJ/m
	22	6pm	One Serg. and 70 men detrained at 3 a.m. and proceeded by route march to MOUSSOT Camp (MUSSO)	WJ/m

Army Form C. 2118.

WAR DIARY
or
INTELLIGENCE SUMMARY.
(Erase heading not required.)

Instructions regarding War Diaries and Intelligence Summaries are contained in F.S. Regs., Part II. and the Staff Manual respectively. Title pages will be prepared in manuscript.

225TH LONDON FIELD AMBULANCE

Place	Date 1916	Hour	Summary of Events and Information	Remarks and references to Appendices
MARSEILLES (MUSSO)	Nov 22	6pm	Party at LA VALENTINE (two Lieut. H.M. LAMBERT, 70 O.R., 67 animals and 3 vehicles) and party at Camp CARCASONNE proceeded independently by route march to MUSSOT Camp (MUSSO)	25/fm
			Capt. F. ST. J. STEADMAN, Lieut R.H.S. MARSHALL and 28/fm 7 O.R. arrived at Camp CARCASONNE	26/fm 25/fm
	23	6pm	Capt STEADMAN and party as above arrived at MUSSO Camp	
	25	6pm	Revd Lt. McKINLEY, C.F. to attached to this unit for rations and accommodation as from today vice Revd G.F. SHARP, C.F.	25/fm 25/fm
	27	6pm	Serg. ALLGROVE returning from extended leave rejoined the unit today 2305 Pte C. EUNGBLUTT has been admitted to MARSEILLES Stationary Hospital as from 25/11/16 74/044370 Dvr. PALMER, A.F. (A.S.C. attaches) has been admitted to hospital today	25/fm 25/fm 25/fm 25/fm
	28	6pm	Lieut. R. GOVAN (No 2) has been detailed to take medical charge of Transport "CESTRIAN" as from today. He will rejoin unit at port of disembarkation (autd ADMS (LoD.S) leave) The 3 vehicles belonging to this unit landed on board transport "IVERNIA" today The following men having been evacuated sick are struck off the strength:- 74/239975 Pte HOLMES, J.; 74/027496 Pte HILTON, A; 74/215193 Pte ROBINSON, H;	25/fm 25/fm

WAR DIARY

Army Form C. 2118.

2/5TH LONDON FIELD AMBULANCE

Place	Date 1916	Hour	Summary of Events and Information	Remarks and references to Appendices
MARSEILLES (MUSSO)	Nov 28	cont'd 6pm	T4/243592 Dv. BILLINGHAM, J.C.; T4/33729 D' RENTON, R as from 23/11/16; T4/186959 " BOWEN, J ; T4/243591 " BARKER, W R; T4/233565 D'. R PALLISTER T4/243599 D. BROWN, R.W. as from 25/11/16	W5/u
H.M.T. "IVERNIA" at sea		6pm	Seven officers and 2 chaplains and 2 chaplain's batmen (total 280) left MUSSO at 7.45 a/m and proceeded to Docks [march] to Hangar 8 MARSEILLES and embarked at 11 a/m. Voyage started about 5 pm.	W5/u

Appendix F

SECRET

180th INFANTRY BRIGADE.

MARCH TABLE.

18th November 1916.

UNIT.	STRENGTH. O.R.		ANIMALS.	VEHICLES. 4 WHEELED	STARTING POINT.	TIME OF PASSING STARTING POINT.	ROUTE.	APPROX. TIME OF ARRIVAL AT STATION.	TIME OF DEP. OF TRAIN.	NO. OF TRAIN.
	O.	O.R.								
1. Det.1/6th Fd.Co.R.E.	3.	120	-	-	Road junction ¼ mile S of L in BUSSUS BUSSUEL	4.10 a.m.	YAUCOURT – AILLY – LONG – LE CATELET	7.27 a.m.	10.27 a.m.	No.16 T.C.
2. Rem.1/6th Fd.Co.R.E.	3.	115	27	-	-do-	8.25 a.m.	-do-	11.17 a.m.	2.17 p.m.	No.17 Special
3. Det.2/5th Fd.Amb.	3	120	-	-	-do-	8.25 a.m.	-do-	11.17 a.m.	2.17 p.m.	-do-
4. 2/19th Bn Lon. Rgt.	39	958	24	1	AILLY LE HAUT CLOCHER cross roads.	9.20 a.m.	LONG – LE CATELET.	11.17 a.m.	2.17 p.m.	-do-
5. Rem.2/5th Fd.Amb.	8	289	67	3	Road junction ¼ mile E of L in BUSSUS BUSSUEL	11.40 a.m.	YAUCOURT – AILLY – LONG – LE CATELET.	2.27 p.m.	5.27 p.m.	No.18 T.C.
6. H.Q. 180 Inf.Bdo.	7	40	20	-	Road junction S.E. end of GORENFLOS.	4.10 p.m.	BRUCAMPS – VAUCHELLES – LA FOLIE – L'ETOILE – CONDE.	6.27 p.m.	9.27 p.m.	No 19 Special
7. 2/20th Bn Lon.Rft.	39	958	24	1	Cross roads YAUCOURT BUSSUS	3.50 p.m.	AILLY – LONG – LE CATELET.	6.27 p.m.	9.27 p.m.	No. 19 Special

www.ingramcontent.com/pod-product-compliance
Lightning Source LLC
Chambersburg PA
CBHW081429160426
43193CB00013B/2232